TV Laughtermakers

ANTHONY DAVIS

Boxtree

First published in 1989 by Boxtree Limited
Published in association with Independent
Television Books Ltd

Text copyright © Anthony Davis 1989

Designed by Dave Goodman
Typeset by Action Typesetting Ltd, Gloucester
Printed and bound in Italy by OFSA S.p.a.,
Milan

For Boxtree Limited,
36 Tavistock Street,
London.
WC2E 7PB

British Library Cataloguing in Publication
Data
Davis, Anthony, *1927 –*
 T.V. laughtermakers.
 1. Television Comedy
 programmes.
 Performances. Biographies – Collections
 I. Title
 791.45'092'2

ISBN 1 – 85283 – 236 – 3

ACKNOWLEDGEMENTS

The author and publishers gratefully
acknowledge the assistance of the TV Times
Picture Library and the following companies
for use of pictures:
ABC TV; BBC Enterprises Ltd; Channel 4;
LWT; Universal Pictorial Press.

Page 1
★ John Cleese, the funniest man in the world,
according to American comedian Steve Martin ★

Page 2
★ Sid James, the homely-faced comic actor from
South Africa, who died in 1976 ★

CONTENTS

★

	Introduction	6
1	Stand and Deliver	8
2	Two of a Kind	16
3	Men in Skirts	28
4	The Outrageous Ones	38
5	Sitcom Comics	52
6	Made by Radio	60
7	Out of Uniform	74
8	Palladium Nights	82
9	The Electronic Age	88
10	New Talent	96
11	The Oxbridge Revolution	104
12	The Graduates II	110
13	Creating an Impression	116
14	Comic Actors	122
15	Comic Actresses	140
16	The New Wave	146
	Index	158

INTRODUCTION

I believe humour contributes to well-being. I don't know anybody who thinks about their overdraft when they're laughing, do you? **SPIKE MILLIGAN**

Wanting to be loved is what gets you started as a comedian. The most difficult thing is keeping that feeling – to want to go on stage, to want all those people laughing. **JIM DAVIDSON**

Comedy is the hardest profession in the world. It is also the most overpopulated facet of show business. There are hundreds of good comics hoping to make a breakthrough – despite the fact that there isn't much room at the top. **ROY WALKER** (right)

We laugh at all manner of things: funny faces, funny voices, funny clothes and funny predicaments. We laugh at jokes and puns, witticisms and insults, at people slipping on banana skins or being deluged with water, at impersonations of the famous, and men masquerading as women.

Psychologists tell us we need laughter to defuse tensions within us. It helps us get rid of our hang-ups. Jokes about mothers-in-law siphon off aggressive feelings, and we laugh at the misfortunes of others in relief that they did not happen to us. Humour smoothes the rough edges of human relationships at work and in the home.

The things we laugh at have not changed in thousands of years. Greeks and Romans had blue jokes and puns. Eric Sykes says: 'In Egyptian times people laughed when someone got hit on the head by a stone falling off the Pyramid, or stubbed his toe on a palm tree or fell in the Nile.'

Nevertheless, TV comedy has changed over the years. In the early days it was found mainly in 'variety' bills along with acrobats and jugglers, singers and musicians. On the day the BBC began the world's first regular service in 1936 it screened a programme called simply *Variety,* which featured Buck and Bubbles, coloured American cross-talk comedians and dancers. ITV, on its opening night in 1955, also had a programme called *Variety,* which included Reg Dixon, Derek Roy and Harry Secombe. In these programmes the top of the bill act, usually a comedian or singer, appeared only at the end of the programme.

Variety gave way to 'the show', in which the star acts as host throughout the programme, joining guests in an integrated entertainment. But the range of comedy programmes is today much wider. Not only are there sketch shows and situation comedies; TV laughtermakers today include impressionists, game show hosts and commentators on the ridiculous, such as

Denis Norden in *It'll be Alright on the Night.*

Whether modern comedy is funnier is arguable, though memories tend to make the past seem better perhaps than it was. Certainly there is more comedy today than ever before, and comics have more to say. Targets of humour have progressed beyond wives and mothers-in-law to politicians and heads of state. Some comedy has become anarchic, some involves TV technology. Some has become sharp-edged and political, though topical humour tends not to pay as well. It is also rarer on TV since programmes are often taped long before transmission and little is now live.

In fact, material is not as important as delivery. Eric Morecambe's catch phrases were not particularly funny in themselves. His artistry made them so. As Frank Carson says of his gags: 'It's the way I tell 'em.' But joke telling is only part of comedy. Some funny men, like Peter Cook, rarely tell jokes.

Jimmy Tarbuck has told me: 'There are two factions of comedians; there are funny men, and men who say funny things.' As examples he cited Tommy Cooper as a funny man, Bob Hope as a man who says funny things – and Eric Morecambe as one of the few men who was both.

There are other possible categories. Some comics originate their own comedy; others rely on writers. Some are happy to perform solo; others prefer to work in a team. Some are aggressive and rude, others are diffident or camp. There are comics who are versatile and accomplished actors – as Ronnie Barker was – while others always play the same part – as Tony Hancock did. There are also actors who are good comics. Some of the greatest laughtermakers are, indeed, actors who hate to be described as comics, even though they have become identified with particular comedy roles, as Warren Mitchell is with Alf Garnett.

Once comics came to television from music hall and radio, then from working men's clubs and pubs, but since the Sixties new ideas and developments have tended to come from graduates who began in university revues. Many comics turned to comedy as children as a form of protection against schoolmates. For example, Dudley Moore has told me: 'It was my smallness that made me take up comedy at school, playing comic parts in plays. I thought, "They'll laugh at me anyway. I'll make them laugh *with* me, laugh when I want them to laugh."' Many of them – and this is not confined to impressionists – began by impersonating pop stars or schoolmasters at school.

These various types, along with others, are represented in this book; but it would be impossible to deal with *all* television's popular laughter raisers, which is why readers may find some of their own favourites have been omitted. The reason that few women are mentioned is because, comparatively, there are not many in the laughter business. Some consider this is because men are unwilling to accept them, though Victoria Wood says: 'There are so few of us because women lack confidence.' However, attitudes seem to be changing.

7

STAND AND DELIVER

★

Stand-up comics are the bravest of the laughtermakers, presenting comedy in its most elemental form. They go before audiences single-handed, defying them not to laugh. Not for them the support of a partner, or a company in which to shelter; on occasion they may work as part of a team in sketches, but basically they work alone.

There are not so many of them plying their trade now – on TV, at least – many established ones having turned to hosting quizzes and game shows. This is a role for which a comedian's confidence, repartee and ad-libbing are well-suited, and it does not use up material like conventional performances.

The stand-up comics have much in common, for they do the same job, but they are different in their approach, in methods and as persons – as can be seen by considering four of the best.

Frankie Howerd

'Ladies and gentlemen. I was amazed. No, don't laugh, titter ye not. No, listen. . . .' That is a typical opening to a Frankie Howerd monologue. He alternately coaxes and berates his audience. He dithers. The face, which has been likened to that of a weary camel, becomes tortured. 'Let's get myself comfy,' he says, wriggling as if adjusting an imaginary corset as he begins his address.

He may be rude about his accompanist. 'Poor old thing, she'll have to go. She's past it, poor soul. No, don't laugh. Don't mock the afflicted.' On royal gala occasions his traditional target is impresario Lord Delfont. On one occasion Howerd assured the audience Delfont had personally done the flower arrangements in the royal box – because the previous year he had found they were one rose short. Delfont was also his butt on *The Frost Programme* in 1966 when Howerd was describing a West End revue in which he was starring:

'The thing was, you see, I wanted to make this into a kind of sophisticated, satirical show. I mean, of course, well, you know Bernard Delfont put this show on, and I went to him and I said, "We must have something, you know . . . good" and – well, no, you see, he's a bit common. Well, no, a bit like you actually. I went to Bernard Delfont and I said, "Look, let's have something, you know, more sophisticated," you see.

'So he said to me: "What we must have is nudes. Bags of nudes," he said, "all over the stage. Wherever you look." "Well," I said, "Bernie," I said, "you can't have that in these modern days," I said. "That's old-fashioned. They've seen all that." Well, at least I have, I'll tell you. Well, no, you see, I mean the thing is, I've done a lot of these shows. You know, those sort of the naked and the dead. I've seen all those. I mean, after all, twice nightly for two and a half years is too much for any man, you know.

'So I said, "No," I said. I said to Bernard Delfont, "It's no good being common; you've got to be sophisticated," I said. Well, no, you can't, can you? No good being common. So I said, "If we've got to have a bit of bare flesh let's be sophisticated about it, you know, smart," I said. "Let's get that nice girl who sings in her bare feet." So that's how Cilla and I got together.'

And so he went on, apparently rambling, actually delivering a rehearsed performance.

When I first met him more than 20 years ago in his dressing room in a London theatre he turned a baleful glare on a photographer, whom he had not been expecting. 'If I know I'm going to be photographed I usually wash or put on something decent, otherwise I look about 150,' he grumbled. 'I'm not one of those who likes action photographs – three chins and bags of expression. I like pretty-pretty photographs

★ 'No, don't laugh, titter ye not.' It's that morose bumbler, Frankie Howerd ★

that make me look young. I'm not concerned with looking full of personality. I like to be *drooled* over. All right, all right, you can take some, but they'll print the most ugly; they always do.'

More than once he apologised: 'I'm sorry I don't come out with anything witty.' He explained: 'People are fooled into thinking I'm funny offstage. I'm not. I wish I was. I wish I was a Harry Secombe, but I rely on writers to be funny. When I'm off duty there is no conscious effort on my part to be a funny man. Why should there be? I'm a professional. You don't expect a professional, once he's turned off from work, to go on doing it. You wouldn't expect it of a banker, an accountant or a shipbuilder, would you? Of course not. But when you're a comedian people expect you to be funny all the time, otherwise they think of you as pathetic and lonely.'

Though Howerd works from scripts and rarely ad-libs, he reshapes gags, emphasises words, and senses and uses audience reaction. 'What I try to do is give the impression of being spontaneous. It's acting. I don't write scripts – I wish I could – though I occasionally contribute ideas and situations. When I get my script I try it out at home and I learn it and I learn it. It's only when I've learned the words and repeated them time and time again that gradually the act comes to life, and when I know it well enough it comes out of me as if it was part of me, I hope.'

He sometimes memorises scripts walking streets near his London home at night, and recalls how, on one occasion, the woman occupant of a house in a square dialled 999 complaining that a suspicious character had passed by several times, muttering to himself and gesticulating. A police car arrived. 'Oh, it's you,' said the officers, recognising him. He has also rehearsed before cattle in fields near his West Country retreat. 'A terrible audience,' he says morosely.

Francis Alex Howerd was born in York in 1922 but brought up in Woolwich. His father was in the regular army but died when the boy was only three, and his mother, left to bring up three children, went out charring to supplement her pension. Howerd was a nervous boy with a stutter but he joined a church dramatic society and gave his first public performance at 13 in Ian Hay's play *Tilly of Bloomsbury,* playing Tilly's father in a beard. He says he was so tense he was incoherent; now he capitalises on the stutter and puts it on, but then it arose when he was nervous.

At 18 he auditioned for RADA, declaiming Shakespeare, but by his own account was gauche and suburban and lost his nerve. When RADA rejected him he wept, abandoned thoughts of becoming an actor and decided to be a comic. He auditioned for Carrol Levis talent contests but was turned down and settled to work as a junior in an insurance office in London's dockland.

When World War Two began, Howerd joined the Royal Artillery and then tried to switch to a forces entertainment unit as a comic; but he went to pieces at auditions and was rejected both by Stars in Battledress and ENSA.

Nevertheless, he managed to develop a patter act in less formal shows in canteens and barrack rooms. He did hundreds of such shows during the war and learned to control his stammer. The bumbling manner grew and he felt comfortable with it.

After the war ex-sergeant Howerd appeared in a troop show at the Stage Door Canteen, was seen by an agent and given his first professional booking in a road show called *For the Fun of It.* At the Sheffield Empire he shared bottom place on the bill with Max Bygraves. (Donald Peers and Nosmo King were the top names.) That was when he changed the spelling of his surname from the commonplace Howard with an 'a' to Howerd with an 'e'. This was mainly because show business had so many Howards – among them Michael, Trevor, Leslie and Sydney – but also because he thought, shrewdly, that people would suspect a misprint and remember the name.

He broke into radio in *Variety Bandbox* with Derek Roy, his first joke on the air being about a visitor to a zoo who saw another man trying to move an elephant by pushing it. It wouldn't budge so the first man gave him a hand. It still would not budge. The first man said: 'This is ridiculous. You should find the keeper.' The second man said: 'I'm trying to – he's under the elephant.'

He spun it out into a five-minute routine. By then he was putting in all the 'oohs' and 'aahs' and dithering to fill time. He was still writing his own material because he could not afford writers, but then Eric Sykes, a rep actor at the time, sent him a script. Sykes went on to write for Howerd for years.

By the early Fifties Howerd was established. So were his catch phrases: 'Please yourselves' (when audience reaction was less than whole-hearted), 'Shut your face' (to any real or imaginary interrupter) and, 'And the best of luck.' This was first said as a soprano launched herself at a high C in radio's *Variety Bandbox.* Later it became 'And the best of *British* luck.'

In 1953 he starred in *Dick Whittington* at the London Palladium, and a year later appeared in his first film, *The Runaway Bus,* and played Bottom in *A Midsummer Night's Dream* at the Old Vic in front of the Queen. But there were bad years as the Fifties turned to the Sixties. It was the era of pop music. Music halls closed, situation comedies dominated TV, and he suffered concussion when he fell from a horse. At a low ebb, he considered taking a pub, but in 1962 he was booked to appear at the Establishment club in Soho among the new wave of satirists. Johnny Speight wrote his script, in which he derided the company he was in. That led to a booking on *That Was the Week That Was* in which he commented on Reginald Maudling's 1963 Budget, overran by several minutes and scored a triumph. Howerd was rediscovered.

He went on to star in 1966 in the musical, *A Funny Thing Happened on the Way to the Forum,* in his first Royal Variety Performance and in the film *The Great St Trinian's Train Robbery,* followed by *Carry On Doctor, Carry On Up the Jungle, Up the Chastity Belt* and *Up the Front.*

In 1970 he made the BBC series *Up Pompeii,* later a film. Howerd played Lurcio, a put-upon but belligerent slave. When his master, Ludicrus Sextus, boasted that his daughter Erotica was 'so delightfully chaste,' Howerd replied with a leer: 'And so easily caught up with.' The series had public baths, orgies and Christians fed to lions, and was a mixture of low comedy and high camp. 'When I saw the first script for *Up Pompeii* I thought it was very vulgar,' he says, 'very vulgar indeed. Then I decided it was in the tradition of British music hall – with the comic wearing a toga. But offensive, no. In a way it's like the *Carry On* films.'

He has twice been chosen as the Variety Club's Show Business personality, and has been awarded the OBE.

Ken Dodd

Ken Dodd is the comedians' comedian. When *The Observer Magazine* polled 13 star comedians in 1988 asking who they found seriously funny, only one comic received more than a single vote. He was Dodd, who was chosen by four of them – Victoria Wood, Tom O'Connor, Bernard Manning and Bob Monkhouse, who called him 'Simply the best there is.'

Dodd himself declined to name a living comedian. 'Today there are many fine British comedians but I think it is invidious to name names since most of them work in the House of Commons.' However, he admitted to having admired Tommy Handley, Ted Ray and Arthur Askey.

Dodd has hair that would serve for a loo brush – or would have done before it thinned – and teeth like a garden rake – the legacy of an accident on a bike when he was 12 and hit the pavement with his face. He sometimes speculates whether he would have become a star if the teeth had been straightened. His main prop is his 'tickling stick', a feather duster that he brandishes. 'How are you diddling?' is his greeting, 'Tatty bye' his farewell.

'What a lovely day for going to Trafalgar Square, throwing a bucket of whitewash over the pigeons and saying "See how you like it,"' he declares. 'What a lovely day for pushing a cucumber through the vicar's letter box and shouting "The Martians have landed."' In full flow he can carry an audience with him in inspired flights of lunatic fancy, throwing in one liners like: 'Ladies … if you want your husband to stop eating between meals – hide his false teeth,' and 'She was only a barber's daughter – but sometimes she gets very stroppy.' He will strum frantically on a banjo and announce 'By jove, I needed that.'

His inventions include the Knotty Ash jam-butty trees, black pudding plantations, snuff quarries, treacle wells and broken biscuit repair works, Professor Chuckabutty, the operatic tenor and sausage-knotter, and, most famously, the midget Diddymen (Nigel Ponsonby-Smallpiece, Wee Hamish, Little Evans, Dicky Mint and the rest) played on stage by children.

'Diddy' was an old expression in the Dodd family used to describe diminutive relatives. His act is salted with other Doddisms including 'tattifalarious' and 'discomknockerating'. When he was awarded the OBE in 1981 he was reported as saying: 'I am delighted and full of plumptiousness. The jam butty workers are discomknockerated and the Diddymen are diddy-delighted.'

The main reason he has not appeared more often on television is that he likes to take time to warm up, and more time to develop his flights of fancy. He has the reputation of being almost impossible to get off stage when in his stride.

He was born in 1927 in Knotty Ash, Liverpool, and started when a boy as a ventriloquist with a doll called Charlie Brown. When he left school at 14 he went into his father's coal business, and sold hardware from the back of a van. He also appeared in concert parties and turned professional in 1954.

When he made his debut at the London Palladium in 1965 he was apprehensive whether the south would accept him, but he stayed 42 weeks and set box office records. He went on to pack venues like Blackpool's great Opera House. A few years ago he vowed to play every live theatre in the country and discovered that there are so many he may never complete the task, despite travelling 60,000 miles a year.

'Practically every town has a civic theatre and I'm pleased to say that there are more popping up every year. I think it's marvellous that everyone gets a chance to see live theatre because it has no equal. By jove, it's not every

★ 'How are you diddling, missus?' The comedians' comedian, the man from Knotty Ash, Ken Dodd in full flight, with, as always, his tickling stick ★

day that you get an opportunity to see Doddy's tickling stick in its full glory.

'There's nothing like a good laugh for airing the lungs, blowing the fluff off the chuckle muscles and giving the old ego a boost. I don't mind people being miserable when they come to see one of my shows, but they're not allowed out again unless they are laughing.'

He keeps books of jokes and how well or badly they have fared with audiences in different localities, and can quote Freud, Kant and Schopenhauer in support of his theories about comedy, though he says, 'The trouble with Freud was that he never played second house on a Friday night at the Glasgow Empire.'

As a ballad singer he had hit records in the Sixties including *Love Is Like a Violin*, *Happiness* and *Tears*. Unusually in show business, he has not made any secret of his political views. 'I think Margaret Thatcher has given this country back its pride,' he says. But little is known about his private life beyond the fact that he has had two long engagements – without marrying. He says simply: 'The public don't have a warrant to know everything about me.'

Dave Allen

Unlike Howerd and Dodd, Dave Allen does not appear anyone's idea of a comic. He is well-groomed, dresses neatly and conservatively, and usually looks serious. No one laughs until he talks. 'In case you wonder what I do, I tend to stroll around and chat,' he tells theatre audiences gravely. 'I'd be grateful if you'd refrain from doing the same.'

Actually, he is not so much a stand-up comedian as a sit-down one. Probably the image most viewers have of him is perched on a high stool, whisky in one hand, a Gauloise in the other (before he stopped smoking). 'The stool is there because I got tired of standing up, and with everyone out in the audience having a drink, I thought I might as well have one. On television it works out very conveniently because you aren't moving and they can get the camera shots right more easily.'

Half the first finger of his left hand is missing, lost in a car door in his youth. He sometimes draws attention to its loss with the words, 'Comic with 9½ fingers.' Allen has a highly developed sense of the absurd. 'Do you know that in New York the traffic lights *tell* you what

to do. "**WALK . . . DON'T WALK.**" People walk across the road who don't want to. They obey an order, "**WALK.**" But the inference is you're an idiot. I think if a machine tells you what to do it should be courteous: I *advise* you not to walk.'

However, Allen, whose customary farewell is 'Goodnight, good luck and may your god go with you,' is identified mainly with stories about drunks and religion. Example: 'To test whether a watch is shockproof I shout at it: "The Pope's a transvestite."' Allen points out: 'I talk also about all sorts of things, but it's the religion and drunks they remember.'

David Tynan O'Mahony was born in Dublin in 1936, the son of a newspaper executive, and was educated by Catholic priests. He left home to work as junior reporter on a small provincial paper, but got a boat to England in 1955 and became a Redcoat at a holiday camp like many other comics before and since. His first attempt at comedy was an impersonation of Dean Martin and Jerry Lewis. 'I felt that if the act didn't go over, the audience would blame Martin and Lewis,' he says.

Eventually he got a booking at a working men's club. The fee was 10 shillings and his fares came to 5s 6d. His patter: 'I went to see a psychiatrist. He said, "Stand by a window and stick your tongue out." I said, "Why?" He said, "I don't like the fellow across the street." I asked him, "Do I have an inferiority complex?" He said, "No, you're just inferior."'

Nobody cheered. Nobody booed. They just sat, but he was then on a bill in Newcastle-upon-Tyne with Val Doonican, and when the singer got his first TV series he asked to use Allen, who did a four-minute spot sitting on a stool and became resident comedian in the series.

His own classic *Tonight with Dave Allen* series began in 1967. He interspersed monologues with filmed sketches with a regular team, recording up to 300 for each six-week run. Sometimes the humour was bleak. There were sketches about nuclear war and the end of civilisation. More popular were those in period costume as Richard III, Sherlock Holmes or Robin Hood.

A typical Robin Hood gag had Little John greeting him: 'Why, hello Robin, nice morning. What you carrying under your arm?'

★ Dave Allen, above, demonstrates that he does sometimes work in a standing position. Jasper Carrott, right, used to have long hair and play guitar, but both hair and guitar have featured less with the passing of the years ★

Robin says: 'What, this? This is a gun.'

'A gun Robin. What's a gun?'

'It kills things. This is a Winchester repeating rifle. Ah, a deadly weapon, this is. They do say it's going to make the arrow obsolete.'

'Show us how it works, Robin.'

Robin puts the rifle against his bow like an arrow, pulls back the cord and lets fly. The rifle hits the ground a few feet in front of him. His men watch in silence. Then Little John says unenthusiastically: 'Very nice, Robin. I must get one of them.'

Jasper Carrott

Balding and staring-eyed, Jasper Carrott has been likened to a cross between a goldfish and a melancholy weasel. His facial expressions range from pop-eyed bewilderment to chinless incomprehension, and he laughs at his own jokes. He is another sit-down comic, usually seen on a stool in open-necked shirt and sports jacket.

His monologues move from being heightened versions of the way men talk in pubs to diatribes about political and environmental stupidities. A frequent target is *The Sun* news-

'Jasper who?' he was asked.

'Carrott,' he answered, for no good reason.

He left school at 16 with two O-levels and his first job was as a travelling salesman of denture paste. At 25 he borrowed £50 from a friend and opened a folk club in Solihull called The Boggery. He acted as MC and also sang. His influences were Tom Lehrer and Mort Sahl. At 30 he had his first hit record, *Funky Moped.* The flip side was a spoof of *Magic Roundabout,* the show for tinies. ('You lousy old flea bag,' said Florence. 'Call yourself a dog. I've seen better hair on a lavatory brush.') This was a monologue he had recorded privately two years earlier at the Boggery and which was banned on radio as risqué. His records went on to earn him three gold and three silver discs, but on stage the introductions to his songs got longer until he stopped bothering to sing.

The introductions developed into monologues about his life and hobbies such as football, but stardom and a different lifestyle eventually made it difficult for him to continue in that vein, and in 1982 came a change. 'I discovered I could write with other people and I had a hell of a lot to say that, underneath, was making me very angry,' he says. He insists he will not compromise and would play to a small audience in a theatre if he lost his TV audience of millions.

In 1984 he travelled to America where he was unknown, and competed against American comics in 'open mike' nights, either unpaid or for paltry fees, dying some deaths but also scoring some successes. Offstage, he says he has become quieter. He does not tell stories all the time, and finds the comedy business unnatural. 'I've always been a reluctant performer and am totally dissatisfied with everything,' he says.

His new interests are alternative medicine and metaphysics (the branch of philosophy concerned with the nature of existence and of truth and knowledge). His interest in alternative medicine stems from a period of illness eventually attributed to a wheat allergy, and the metaphysics, he says, 'to passing 40'.

He still lives in Birmingham, declines to appear on chat and quiz shows and does not open supermarkets. He says he cannot be funny in those circumstances. He never seeks publicity and insists: 'I'm as boring as old paste.' It is patently untrue.

paper, and he can also be rude about its readers, which is bold of him since millions of them are likely to be among his viewers. He says that there is more to comedy than telling an hour of jokes. 'I believe comedy should have some sort of point. Comedy for me has to be edgy, dangerous. It has to be. Taking people to task, naming names, that's the danger area now.'

In series including *Carrott's Lib* and *Carrott Confidential* he has performed live, and prefers live television. 'I like to be topical because I am a very concerned member of the human race,' he says, though he adds that he is 'one of those wishy-washy people who sees all sides of a problem'. This is not always apparent.

He was born Bob Davies, son of an engineer, in Birmingham in 1945, but was nicknamed Jasper at school. 'Now Bob Davies doesn't exist,' he says. 'Nobody ever calls me Bob.' Even his wife calls him Jasper. He added Carrott himself at 17 on a golf course when he was introduced to another player with the words, 'This is Jasper.'

TWO OF A KIND

The classic double act of the music halls consisted of a straight man or 'feed' and a clown. The straight man would endeavour to tell a story, recite a monologue or sing, while interrupted by the clown – traditionally with the words, 'I say, I say, I say!', leading to a riddle or joke, to which the straight man would snap, 'I don't wish to know that.' and 'Kindly leave the stage.'

On television the roles of straight man and comic have become less clear cut; some duos have interchanged them. But in most double acts the partners depend on each other, and as they may spend more time together than with their marriage partners it helps if they are on good terms. This is not always the case. Laurel and Hardy, Abbott and Costello, Jerry Lewis and Dean Martin, even Lucan and McShane (the married couple who played Old Mother Riley and her daughter Kitty) quarrelled. Morecambe and Wise, the most acclaimed of television's double acts, did not, though (or perhaps, because) they never lived in each other's pockets and offstage led their own lives.

Morecambe and Wise

They were the most loved British comics of the television age – loved in all sections of society. It became fashionable for distinguished actors and actresses to appear on TV in 'the Eric and Ernie show'. Dame Flora Robson, Sir Michael Redgrave, Eric Porter, Sir Ralph Richardson and Vanessa Redgrave were among those who did. Glenda Jackson played Cleopatra in a sketch, delivering the line: 'The men worship my feet. . . . They don't think much of my face but my feet are having a marvellous time.'

Newsreader Angela Rippon flashed her legs in a dance number and was a national sensation. André Previn was induced to leap into the air while conducting the orchestra in Grieg's piano concerto so that Morecambe, at

the piano, could see him over the lid and know when to start playing. Shirley Bassey sang *Smoke Gets In Your Eyes* straight-faced while Morecambe and Wise prised her foot from a hole in a staircase, and replaced her high-heeled sandal with an army boot. Even former Prime Minister Harold Wilson (now Lord Wilson of Rievaulx) appeared in a sketch in 1976. Wise recalls: 'He said, "Don't give me too many lines", and then added gags of his own. He was very good.' But no one ever came badly out of a Morecambe and Wise programme.

Their Christmas Day shows were an institution. One had newsreaders and presenters of documentary programmes appearing to cartwheel and somersault effortlessly in numbers from *South Pacific.* The audience for their Christmas Day show in 1977 on BBC1 was put at 28 million.

Morecambe was born Eric Bartholomew in 1926, but adoped the name of the Lancashire resort that was his birthplace. Wise was born Ernest Wiseman in Leeds in 1925. They met as 13-year-olds in 1939 when Morecambe went for an audition for *Youth Takes a Bow,* Bryan Michie's child discovery show. He wore a cutdown tailcoat and dress trousers, a bootlace tie and a beret, and sucked a lollipop. He did impressions of Bud Flanagan and Fred Astaire and, in blackface, G.H. Elliott, 'the chocolate coloured coon'.

Presiding at the audition in a Manchester cinema was impresario Jack Hylton. Sitting beside him was Wise, only five months older than Morecambe, but already under contract and earning twice as much as his father, a railway porter, with whom he had performed a double act at the age of eight. (Wise's part was

★ **Morecambe and Wise (with Ernie's allegedly short fat hairy legs partially on view) in one of their ITV shows of the Sixties ★**

a clog dance.) Morecambe joined the touring show and by 1941 he and Wise had a double act, but the show was disbanded in 1942 and they went separate ways – Morecambe to be a Bevin boy in the mines. They were reunited by chance in 1947 when Morecambe joined Sanger's Circus and found himself a feed to the resident comic, Wise.

They started as conventional cross-talk comics, modelling their act on that of America's Abbott and Costello, in which Bud Abbott was a bullying straight man, Lou Costello the fat, funny half. Originally Wise was the butt of Morecambe's jokes but over the years the situation was reversed and it was more often Morecambe who was tricked.

Their first TV series, *Running Wild,* in 1954, was unsensational, but in *The Morecambe and Wise Show* on ITV from 1961 they established routines to which they were to adhere. Wise promised each week that Morecambe could have a big acting role as Fagin or Jekyll and Hyde or Abraham Lincoln and Morecambe got into costume only to hear Wise declare: 'But we've run out of time.' Another running gag had them opening a door at the end of the show to encounter a blank brick wall, a custard pie in the face, or a train rushing towards them.

It was in this series that they adopted *Two of a Kind,* a Johnny Mercer number which became one of their themes. Their timing was a joy to watch as they exploited mundane material with inspired improvisation within well-rehearsed routines.

In 1968 Morecambe suffered a heart attack and their activities were suspended. After his recovery they crossed channels to the BBC and Eddie Braben replaced Dick Hills and Sid Green as their scriptwriter. Their dance routines were less energetic as a result of Morecambe's illness but they made simple routines into classics. There were domestic sketches, in some of which they were seen sharing a double bed. No one was apparently bothered by this. There were also Wise's 'plays what I have wrote'.

'Good evening, ladies and gentlemen, and welcome to the show,' was Wise's standard opening to the shows, which were rich in catch phrases, most of them spoken by Morecambe: 'You can't see the join' (referring to the wig Morecambe alleged Wise wore, but did not), 'Short, fat, hairy legs' (referring to

Wise's lower limbs), 'Just watch it, that's all', 'Pardon?', 'I'll smash your face in', 'Good evening, young sir' (usually to an actress), 'Arsenal', 'I just said that', 'Get out of that. You can't, can you?' (applying a necklock), 'This boy's a fool' (as Wise fell for a scheme) and 'There's no answer to that' (in response to a double entendre). Their Antony and Cleopatra sketch with Glenda Jackson in 1971 introduced 'What do you think of it so far?' with the answer, 'Rubbish!'

Their exit was a kind of hornpipe dance, hands behind backs. Other visual gags included Morecambe catching an imaginary stone in a paper bag, skewing his spectacles, slapping the back of his neck, hugging Wise's shoulders, and throttling himself as he stood in front of the curtain. Morecambe's two-handed slapping of Wise's face was known to them as 'the slap-face routine'. 'We called it thinking time,' says Wise. 'When he slapped me like that or put his arm round me and called me his little fat friend, that was a pause while we thought, "Help, what comes next?" It gives you confidence, having something physical to do while you think.'

In 1976 both were awarded OBEs and made Freemen of the City of London. Two years later they were lured back to ITV by the promise that they could make films as well as conventional shows, but in 1979 Morecambe suffered another heart attack and underwent surgery. On the day in March when Morecambe left hospital (announcing he planned to be back at work in June) the partners were featured simultaneously at peak time on both major channels. The BBC, continuing a series of repeats under the title *Morecambe and Wise at the BBC,* showed a programme with Magnus Magnusson among the guests, while ITV inserted a repeat of the duo's first show for Thames, with Judi Dench and Donald Sinden.

Despite Morecambe's cheerfulness the 1979 Christmas show had to be cancelled and there was doubt whether they would appear again. They did – but in 1983 Morecambe was ill again, and he died in 1984. Wise, who went solo after Morecambe's death, says: 'We had a great camaraderie. That's where some double acts fall down. They don't talk to each other.'

Cannon and Ball

Cannon and Ball relate with pride that Eric Morecambe told them they would inherit the

★ Morecambe and Wise, television's undisputed favourite double act until Morecambe's death in 1984, after a charity performance ★

★ Cannon and Ball, the double act that Eric Morecambe once tipped to inherit the Morecambe and Wise crown ★

Morecambe and Wise crown. To the extent of becoming the country's most popular double act, this is probably true, though they have not become the institution that Morecambe and Wise were. Possibly no one ever will. Their act is more traditional, Cannon smooth, serious and conscientious, struggling to get things right, Ball in baggy suit, twanging his braces dangerously, as the irresponsible but anxious-to-please kid brother figure.

They came from Oldham, Lancs. Tommy Cannon (born Thomas Derbyshire in 1938) and Bobby Ball (born Robert Harper in 1944) first met in the early Sixties as welders doing repetitious work in an engineering factory. After two impromptu performances at the factory social club they formed a singing partnership, the Harper Brothers. By day they welded and at night, in their best suits, they entertained in Lancashire clubs. Cannon would start singing a romantic ballad. Ball would interrupt with a gag. Gradually the comedy content became stronger.

After two years they had more club work than they could cope with, though when Ball's cousin, a professional comic, got them a week's booking at a club in Wales it was the first time they had been out of Lancashire. At the end of the week they put in their notices at the factory and went on the road.

They changed their names to Cannon and Ball on a wet morning in a dreary Lancashire café with their manager. 'We got through several pots of tea before someone came up with Cannon and Ball,' says Cannon. 'We decided those names fitted us perfectly.' As Ball recalls it, his partner picked Cannon after American singer Freddie Cannon, and Ball was the natural choice to go with Cannon.

They made the change for their TV debut in *Opportunity Knocks!,* which they still recall with shudders. 'It was a real disaster,' says Cannon. 'We were full of confidence and imagined that stardom was just around the corner. However, our impact was such that we failed to budge the clapometer. We were Opportunity Flops.' This may be understood by resurrecting one of their jokes on the show:

Ball: 'I dreamed last night I was out playing golf with Jack Nicklaus.'
Cannon: 'I had a better dream than that. I dreamed I was in bed with Elizabeth Taylor and Raquel Welch.'

Ball: 'Why didn't you call me?'
Cannon: 'You were out playing golf with Jack Nicklaus.'

'At that time singing was our forte so we set about restructuring the act,' says Cannon. 'Bobby leaned more on his comedy attributes and his scruffy stage image was mirrored by my suave appearance. Since then we've built up the act through our experience as live entertainers but we're not a conventional comedy double act. We try to combine all elements including crosstalk patter, knockabout comedy, pathos and of course singing.'

Their first series was ITV's *The Wheeltappers' and Shunters' Social Club* in 1974, after which they were booked for a regular spot on *Bruce Forsyth's Big Night* in 1978, but were crowded out week after week. When they were given their own series it was hit by an ITV strike. 'Cannon and Blackout' they styled themselves, but finally *The Cannon and Ball Show* got on screen. 'Rock on, Tommy!' cried Ball.

In a 13-week tour in 1983 they played 134 shows in 45 theatres, and at the Dominion Theatre in London they broke its all-time record with £650,000 in advance bookings. They made their film debut in a police comedy, *The Boys in Blue,* though they were no more successful on the big screen than Morecambe and Wise had been. Nevertheless, they were able to indulge themselves with matching two-tone gold and pale yellow Rolls-Royces until they decided these were too ostentatious. Offstage, they go their own ways, as Morecambe and Wise did.

Little and Large

Their close rivals, Little and Large, also began as singers in pubs in 1960, turning to comedy before appearing on *Opportunity Knocks!* in 1971 – and winning.

Straight man Syd Little, only 5 ft 5 in tall and 9 stone in weight, and virtually blind without his glasses, was born Cyril Mead in Blackpool in 1942, son of an electrician. By the time he was 14 his family had moved to Manchester where he used money earned on a paper round to buy a plastic, four-stringed 'Welcome to Britain, Elvis Presley' guitar priced £1.20. (Presley was expected to come to Britain, but never did.) A year later he moved on to a six-string model and began entertaining in local pubs. He played modern numbers while his father played old ones on a concertina. Then he bought an electric guitar and became a regular at the Stonemason's pub at Timperley.

Eddie Large, 5 ft 4 in and 15 stone, was born McGinnis (Eddie's mother having allegedly changed the name from McGuinness because she was teetotal). He was a sheet metal worker's son, born in Glasgow in 1942, but also moved to Manchester as a boy. His first ambition was to be a footballer but he injured a leg in an accident while cycling to work as an electrician.

★ The former Eddie McGinnis and the former Cyril Mead, now better known as Little and Large, who achieved their own television series in the late Seventies ★

Visiting a pub in Timperley with pals, he saw Mead and made a request for *Living Doll.* He then took to standing up with him and joining in songs, and they became a double act, Syd and Friend, though they were still under age to be on licensed premises.

The act developed into Little as a singer and Large as a well-meaning idiot helping him to become a superstar. They played working men's clubs where their names were up in coloured chalk, rather than lights. At one club where they topped the bill they were required to pay admission, and in 1971 they were thinking of quitting when they got on *Opportunity Knocks!* In 1976, after 14 years in show-business, they achieved their own series.

★ Diminutive Scottish raconteur Ronnie Corbett has starred as a stand-up comic and in situation comedy series, but was never more popular than as the smaller of The Two Ronnies ★

The Two Ronnies

The Two Ronnies never adopted the funny man and stooge routine. They swopped the roles, but then they never regarded themselves as a double act; they just worked together in series. They often worked without each other. Barker starred in *Porridge* as old lag Norman Stanley Fletcher, in *Open All Hours* as a stammering, North country shopkeeper, in *The Magnificent Evans* as a Welsh photographer, and in *Clarence* as a short-sighted removal man. Corbett starred in *No, That's Me Over Here,* and *Sorry,* as a man remaining tied to his mother's apron strings, and was also in stage shows,

which Barker avoided. Yet the public regarded them as a double act and they received OBEs from the Queen side by side instead of going up in alphabetical order.

The Two Ronnies always opened with a spoof news routine: 'And in a packed programme tonight...' Then came sketches featuring one or both. Many depended on word-play and some of the best of these were written by Barker under the name Gerald Wiley; one was set in an ironmonger's with Corbett asking for fork handles and being offered four candles. There was generally a film serial, one of the best remembered being *Stop, You're Killing Me,* in which the Ronnies played inept private detectives Piggy Malone and Charley Farley.

A regular feature was a monologue by Corbett, sitting on the edge of a large chair and referring frequently to his 5 ft 1½ inch frame. 'I spent the first six months of my life on a charm bracelet,' he would say. 'I tried to pull up a worm and it got the better of me . . . I did nine holes of golf today – played four and fell down five.' The climax was generally a big musical number in which Barker was often required to appear in drag, though he disliked this. The close was always another news routine with the stars in aggressively patterned or coloured jackets, ending with their traditional sign-off: 'And it's goodnight from me'; 'And it's goodnight from him.'

The shows were packed with double meanings such as 'It's cold enough to freeze the conkers off a horse chestnut tree.' Barker said: 'We all know what it means but a child or your maiden aunt can take the single meaning if they want.'

Before they came together in *The Frost Report* in 1966 their backgrounds were totally different. Corbett's was music hall, Barker's the theatre. Corbett was born in 1930 in Edinburgh, a baker's son, and began taking part in amateur dramatics at 16, but was for two years a civil servant dealing with animal feeding stuffs before his national service in the RAF, during which he became a camp entertainments officer. Afterwards he found engagements in London pubs and clubs, which led him to

★ Before his retirement in 1988, Ronnie Barker, the larger of The Two Ronnies, was also a talented character actor, seen here as the stuttering shopkeeper Arkwright in *Open All Hours* ★

Danny La Rue's club, acting as the drag artist's feed in sketches and playing Napoleon, Caesar and Toulouse-Lautrec. David Frost saw him there, took him to tea at the Ritz and the result was his appearance in *The Frost Report.*

Barker, a year older, was born in Bedford, the son of an oil company clerk. He studied to be an architect but then became a bank cashier. However, after a year in an amateur drama company he turned professional and was in rep in Aylesbury, Manchester and Oxford. In Cardiff on a tour he developed influenza and had to be left behind in bed. He had no money and lived in one room on a loaf and a jug of water for three days. As he caught up with the company in Penzance it went broke; there was not enough money for rail fares home and he had to walk back to Oxford.

After his first London appearance in *Mourning Becomes Electra* at the Arts Theatre, he was in five plays at the Royal Court, including *A Midsummer Night's Dream* and *Lysistrata.* He was billed as Ronald Barker then; he switched to Ronnie because it seemed more friendly when he found work in radio. After comedy shows with Jimmy Edwards, he too was booked for *The Frost Report.*

Corbett and Barker clung together in that series and its successor, *Frost Over England,* because Frost, John Cleese and others in them were from universities while the Ronnies were ex-grammar school boys. Their physical dissimilarities made them an obvious comedy team: the diminutive, twinkling Corbett contrasting with the burly, executive-looking Barker, of whom Corbett said: 'Some people are built like Greek gods; Ronnie B is built like a Greek restaurant.'

The differences between them went beyond appearance. Corbett is a natural entertainer while Barker says: 'I'm not one of those people who can reel off funny story after funny story. I can't ad-lib or be funny to order. I must have a script and a character. That's why I never speak at dinners or open fêtes.'

The Two Ronnies ended (apart from repeats) when Barker retired in 1988, aged 58. He was suffering from high blood pressure and told to avoid stress. He decided to quit at the top and devote himself to his interest in Victoriana – collecting postcards, illustrated books and prints. He left a message on his telephone answering machine: 'Thank you for your

inquiry but I am retiring from public and professional life so I am unable to undertake any more commitments. To those people with whom I have worked I would like to express my gratitude and good wishes. So it's a big thank you from me, and it's goodbye from him. Goodbye.'

Hale and Pace

Gareth Hale and Norman Pace, one of the newest double acts to achieve their own series, have been described as alternative comedians – though not by them. However, they agree, 'We're never going to be end-of-pier comics or do pantomime. It's not an area in which we feel comfortable.'

They began performing as a double act in folk clubs in 1976, Hale originating the majority of the jokes, Pace organising them into sketches, and won notoriety as the two Rons, dinner-jacketed Cockney heavies. The act was born when they were given outsize dinner jackets. 'As soon as we put them on we started talking like East End minders,' says Pace.

They were hailed as the Kray twins of comedy. 'Warm, friendly and psychopathic,' they say. They would threaten people in the front row of the audience with concrete overcoats, and observe menacingly: 'Oh, deary deary me, it's so hard to walk when your legs are broken.' Ron One would ask: 'Do you admire Margaret Thatcher?' and Ron Two would reply: 'It depends if she pays up or not, Ron.' When they performed as the Rons in a Royal Variety show it was regarded as, in their words, 'on the very hem of what people thought acceptable'.

Since then they have wearied of fans greeting them with 'Allo, Ron' and are trying to play down the Rons. 'There's more to us than them,' they say, and point to some of their other

★ Hale and Pace wore dinner jackets when they won notoriety as menacing Cockney heavies named Ron, but they went on to broaden their range with other characterisations ★

characters seen in *Hale and Pace,* their 1988 ITV series, among them the manic presenters of children's programmes, Billy and Johnny. However, their air of menace seems to remain. Some viewers complained about an act in which they announced their intention of microwaving an appealing cat which Hale was stroking – even though the creature, taken from the cooker with the line, 'And here is one which we prepared earlier', was an intentionally obvious fake.

Hale, the one with the moustache, was born in Brixton, and Pace in Newark, Notts. They were both 18 when they met in 1971 at a college of education in Eltham to train as teachers. They groaned when they found they were to share a room because they seemed to have little in common. Pace wore a suit; Hale was long-haired and bearded like a folk singer; but they both became members of Daffy, a five-strong musical comedy group. Their most vivid memory of it was a night at a working men's club in Crayford when they used up all their material in an hour – and found they were expected to fill another hour before the bingo began. They could only perform the act again and were told not to come back.

They worked as PE teachers for about four years and sometimes meet former pupils. 'They say, "You don't remember me", and there's some hairy giant which comes as a shock,' says Hale. 'And that's just the girls,' says Pace inevitably.

Mike and Bernie Winters

Not all partnerships endure. A cautionary story is that of the Winters brothers who, between 1963 and 1972, starred in a series of TV spectaculars, including *The Mike and Bernie Show* and *Mike and Bernie's Music Hall* but split up after nearly a quarter of a century as partners.

Mike was born in 1930, Bernie two years later, in Islington. Their grandfather had come

★ **At the height of their popularity in 1972 Mike and Bernie Winters appeared in an ITV special with actor Kenneth Haigh (centre) as their guest. But the brothers were on the verge of parting company, Mike to move to America, Bernie to embark on a solo career. 'We just came to the end,' says Bernie. 'We were on a treadmill.' They were not the first, and will not be the last, double act to split up ★**

from Russia and the family name was Weinstein. Their father was a small gambler, bookmaker and street fighter.

Mike went to City of Oxford School and later studied clarinet at the Royal Academy of Music. Bernie went from truancy to the stage and never saw a classroom after the age of 12. While still at college, and not yet 17, Mike was invited to play clarinet with a quartet at the Stage Door Canteen, the services entertainment centre. He brought Bernie in on drums and they went on to build an act, including impressions of Lionel Barrymore, Charles Boyer and Ronald Colman. For a time they were part of a Canadian army show unit as musicians and stooges.

They progressed, as Mike put it, from being a couple of unknown failures to a couple of known failures, playing clubs that he described as catering for 'a cross-section of rejects from Alcoholics Anonymous, the SS and the commando section of Millwall Supporters' Club'. At one time they decided to emigrate to Australia and actually filled in the papers, but after their TV debut in *Six-Five Special* they went on to top bills throughout the Sixties.

However, the partnership came under stress and they decided to part. The decision was made five years before the break took effect. Then Mike moved to America to become a businessman, producer and writer, and toothy Bernie set out alone, apart from his dog Schnorbitz, making his solo TV debut in 1978 *Bernie,* going on to host *Whose Baby?* and *Scribble,* and touring as Bud Flanagan in the stage show *Bud and Ches,* with Leslie Crowther.

Bernie said: 'Our temperaments and our outlook on life were completely different and towards the end we began to irritate each other. We just came to the end. We stayed together so long because we were brothers but we'd done all we could as a double act. It became very repetitious. We were on a treadmill and we'd had enough.

'Most double acts don't get on very well. There's a front put up for the public but in 98 per cent of cases there's an undercurrent. It's an unnatural situation being in each other's pockets. A double act is more than a marriage even. You're virtually together 24 hours a day every day. But making the decision to part was extremely hard because we'd been together all our lives.'

MEN IN SKIRTS

★

Men dressed as women have long been part of comedy – though rarely women dressed as men. In most drag acts impersonations are deliberately less than perfect to avoid causing the audience discomfort. Danny La Rue, though playing the most glamorous females, always let audiences know that beneath the glittering dresses and elaborate wigs was a man. Acts such as his have been rare on TV; more commonly men dress up in pantomime dame style. Perhaps the most believable act is that of Hinge and Bracket, whose style is period-dowdy.

Hinge and Bracket

Dr Evadne Mona Hinge and Dame Hilda Nemone Bracket, two slightly dotty elderly spinsters in pince-nez, are devoted to each other and to music. In tea gowns and pearls, and with icing sugar smiles, they sing numbers like *We'll Gather Lilacs* and *Keep the Home Fires Burning,* and although they may send up the songs they do it very gently. They also bicker in a genteel way while sipping sherry and offering meandering reminiscences of Gilbert and Sullivan perform-ances and tours of army camps. Recalling one such tour in Cyprus in the Fifties, entertaining the troops on makeshift stages, Dame Hilda says: 'We had to perform on many shoddy erections.'

George Logan, a former computer pro-grammer, and Patrick Fyffe, a former hair-dresser, have been playing Dr Hinge and Dame Hilda respectively since 1972. They are promo-ted only as Hinge and Bracket, and are rarely photographed out of costume. Probably few of their fans could give their real names. Logan says: 'They know that you're two fellers dressed up but there are some that don't want to be reminded.' In fact, after they have appeared on television, programme journals customarily get letters saying: 'My friend tells me Hinge and Bracket are men. Is this true?'

Detailed biographies are available of the characters. The Dame comes from an old Suffolk family, daughter of Sir Osbert Bracket who left her the family home in Stackton Tressel where she now lives with Dr Hinge. The Doctor comes from an eccentric Scottish family. Her mother remarried a young Mexican architect, her brother Lester ran away to sea, and her sister Lavinia has not spoken to her for 25 years following an accident with a family heirloom.

They met when Dame Hilda was a soprano with the Rosa Charles Opera Company, of which she recalls: 'Quite a number of the founder members were very old. There was a particularly elderly man who helped out backstage and wore a wooden leg actually made from a piece of antique furniture. He used to tap, tap, tap along the corridors in such an amusing way. His leg had a claw and ball foot, you know.'

On their first encounter Dr Hinge fell into a box of chocolates that Dame Hilda had on her lap as she waited for her call to go on stage for a rehearsal of *Carmen.* Dr Hinge had joined the company to understudy the assistant musical director, Herbert van Twinsetmann, who made way for her by falling down a fire escape. 'He used to drink home-made wine,' says Dame Hilda, 'and I well remember Evadne turning him over with her foot, looking up at me and saying, "Hilda, it looks as if I will be on tomorrow."'

In Stackton Tressel they organise the ama-teur opera company, for which Dame Hilda, who enjoyed the reputation of being able to hold a top note for half a minute, sang the soprano role of Mabel in *The Pirates of Penzance.* She sang it 18 times in one week, performing at

★ **Stanley Baxter was at his best in impressions of female Hollywood stars of the Thirties and Forties** ★

2, 5 and 8 pm daily, but this damaged her voice to such an extent she became a contralto.

Dr Hinge occupies the east wing of Dame Hilda's home. She says: 'Dame Hilda's tastes are Louis Quinze; mine are more Louis Armstrong.' Dame Hilda says: 'Neither of us has ever wanted to marry. I have always been too busy and, as I say, if you've never had it you've never missed it.'

Fyffe and Logan are more sparing with information. Fyffe comes from Stafford. His father, mother and an aunt worked the music halls and he enjoyed dressing up as a child, but his first performance in drag was when he held a birthday party at his home. He and two friends had rehearsed an act, miming to Beverley Sisters' records, but the others cried off and he was left to do it on his own. (Since then he has always done his own singing.) He also did impersonations of Eartha Kitt and Marlene Dietrich, and this led to him doing a drag act around Stafford as glamorous Perri St Clair.

He met Logan when they were in the same cabaret and Fyffe's tenor partner quit. Logan, from Glasgow, had trained in music at the Scottish Academy in Glasgow, and although he dropped out after a year, reads music easily.

★ Spinsters in pince-nez, Dr Evadne Hinge and Dame Hilda Bracket, otherwise George Logan and Patrick Fyffe ★

Fyffe, who has never learned, enlisted his help. The original plan was for Logan to wear tails but, surveying Fyffe's wardrobe, he suggested, 'Why don't we do it as two old ladies?' The act was born.

At first they worked largely gay audiences and private parties. 'It was dreadful when we first did it,' Logan says. 'There was no character behind it, just two old ladies singing Gilbert and Sullivan. We didn't have the names Hinge and Bracket then.' However, they had them by the time of *An Evening with Hinge and Bracket* at the 1974 Edinburgh Festival. They moved on into London theatres, records, radio – a strange medium for a largely visual joke – and their own television series, *Dear Ladies*.

Barry Humphries

A more famous television Dame is, of course, Edna Everage, who is a self-styled megastar and looks it. Tall and mauve-haired in, typically, a puce dress with black spots and pink, diamanté-encrusted, winged spectacles, she scatters gladioli to her worshipping fans with a shrill cry of 'Hello possums!' 'This is my little spunky look,' she says, drawing attention to the dress. 'I'm a passionate woman. I have my drives and juices. . . .' The mouth becomes a slit and droops to one side in distaste at audience sniggers.

'You know, the other day my gynaecologist, he looked up and he said, "Edna, how do you give and take so much love?" He's an old gynaecologist with a bit of a tremor, actually, but I think they're the best kind, don't you?'

Barry Humphries's creation is the most extraordinary, outrageous and popular female impersonation in TV history. In *An Audience with Dame Edna* celebrities packed the studio to prompt the Dame with questions, sparking barbed comments and patronising put-downs. She talked of Norm, her husband, prostrate with his prostate, though she has since reported his demise after the switching off of his life support machine. She talked also of her sons, Bruce and Kenny, and her daughter Valmai, who 'goes into supermarkets and, dare I say it, she stuffs frozen chickens down her panti-hose. But the thing is, the store detectives can smell the barbecued chickens as she leaves. She's a human microwave is Valmai.'

In *The Dame Edna Experience* Humphries sent

★ There's nothing like a Dame. Barry Humphries sent up chat shows mercilessly in *An Audience with Dame Edna*. The luckless guest in the lower picture is Sean Connery ★

up chat shows, though Dame Edna was unwilling to accept the term. 'Frankly darlings, I don't think of it as a chat show,' she said before it began. 'Mine will be a form of human intercourse.... There has been a bit of a royal stampede to get on the show and I'm toying with a few of their requests. Princess Michael has very graciously declined, which is sad because I would have adored her. Do you know, darling, I think she's slightly nervous. Her reply revealed a vulnerable side that not many would have perceived. Protocol forbids me to reveal the contents of a 10-page personal letter in two languages but she said she would probably shake on television.'

In the event, stars including Charlton Heston, Sean Connery, Roger Moore and Larry Hagman bravely descended a flight of stairs longer and steeper than on any other show, and with a nurse stationed prominently at the foot. They then suffered the indignity of being required to wear labels bearing their first names for identification. (These were supplied by the Dame's mute assistant, her ageing bridesmaid, Madge.) The opening question to a bemused Larry Hagman was: 'You're used to being interviewed by ordinary, uninteresting people; what's it like to be interviewed by your peer?' Novelist Jeffrey Archer was accused of being boring, and was ejected backwards in his chair through a door in the wall.

Mary Whitehouse, the clean-up TV campaigner, who was an improbable guest, presented Dame Edna with a bunch of gladioli which the star from Moonee Ponds tossed disdainfully into a corner. Whitehouse was enthralled. 'In retrospect it was one of the most enjoyable experiences I've ever had,' she wrote in *TV Times*. 'What was so marvellous was that we had fun without the conversation being full of double-meanings.' This view said much about the niceness of Mary Whitehouse's mind.

Psychiatrist Dr Anthony Clare says: 'The fascination of Edna Everage is that she debunks the pomposity and pretentiousness of the very business she is in.'

Humphries has other personas but Edna's only rival is the claret-nosed, salivating Sir Les Patterson, unofficial cultural attaché to the Court of St James and roving diplomat. Swaying in his booze- and vomit-stained suit, the egregious Sir Les boasts of his amatory exploits: 'I'd fill her up with liquor, check out some doubtful videos, get my cue in the rack, and then – while she's sleeping it off, I'd put in a loving phone call to Lady Patterson.'

Humphries was born in 1934 in Melbourne, a builder's son. He was an art-loving bookworm. 'I stumbled into comedy simply because I found acting in the student revues at Melbourne University more entertaining than studying law,' he says. He failed his exams, then joined a rep company touring Shakespeare while he developed his own act, which by 1956 included Edna Everage, originally a Melbourne housewife who satirised the city's suburban gentility. She was based on female relatives.

He arrived in England in 1959, among a band of talented but wild Australians. One of his diversions was to sup mixed vegetable soup from a sick bag on an airplane. 'If an air hostess sees you it can produce what I call the chain chunder,' he says. 'Five minutes later the pilot is throwing up.'

He appeared in Lionel Bart musicals in the West End. In *Oliver!* he played the undertaker and understudied Ron Moody's Fagin, although he never got to perform the role. Peter Cook invited him to bring his Australian revue characters to the Establishment Club. 'I was put on there one night when Lenny Bruce was too drunk or drugged or dead to appear,' says Humphries. He was not a hit and took to writing scripts for his Barry McKenzie character, the big-chinned, boozing, sex-hungry ocker, whose colourful phrases included 'syphoning the python', 'draining the dragon' and 'making Technicolor yawns'. McKenzie was drawn by Nicholas Garland in *Private Eye* and was the subject of two films, with Humphries playing Edna.

She made her TV debut in a 1968 BBC series *The Barry Humphries Scandals,* with Humphries beginning to create an Australia of kangaroo-hide postcards, marsupial money boxes and ketchup dispensers shaped like gum trees before the world had heard of Paul Hogan. However, the tapes have long since been wiped.

Humphries is clever and sharp and has a well-stocked mind. Offscreen he affects a monocle and favours spotted bow ties and bold-striped double-breasted suits, worn with a wide-brimmed fedora and a fur coat. His second wife is a painter and he has four children.

Dick Emery

In *The Dick Emery Show* in the Sixties and Seventies the most popular of the comic's characters was Mandy, a peroxided man-hunting blonde with the catchphrase: 'Ooh, you are awful – but I like you!' (delivered with a violent push). Mandy was also the star of a 1972 film called *Ooh, You Are Awful*. Another female character in Emery's repertoire was the frustrated, drooping-shouldered, man-hungry Hettie, always clutching a bag and asking males, 'Are you married?'

Actually, men outnumbered women in the Emery rep company – among them a crew-cut bovver boy, a crusty colonel, a bullying traffic warden, an educated tramp, a ton-up motorcyclist, a country yokel, a toothy vicar and the senile Lampwick, who was Emery's favourite. In his last TV programme, a comedy thriller *Jack of Diamonds,* he played a Jewish private eye, Bernie Weinstock, and many other characters. Mandy was not a favourite because she was the least real to him. but she was the one with whom he was identified in the obituaries.

Emery was born into show business in Bloomsbury in 1917. His father and mother, respectively a comedian and a singer, were partners on the halls and Emery attended a different school every week, but his father blew

★ **Dick Emery in the roles of his two most famous women characters, the pushy Mandy (left) and the frustrated Hettie** ★

his money on horses and drink and Emery's parents parted when he was eight. He left school at 15 and was an office boy, a farm hand and a driving instructor until his ambition settled on singing in opera. At 19 he had cards printed, which read: 'Tenor vocalist. Juvenile character parts. Drive any make of car. Sports: football, cricket. Knowledge of guitar. Good torso.'

But then came the war and he joined the RAF and went into its *Gang Show*. In it he started developing his gallery of characters, Mandy among them. After the war he worked up a vicar act and 'dried' while performing it in Brighton. In 1948 he followed Tony Hancock at London's Windmill Theatre, famed for its nudes. He auditioned at 10.30 am and was in his first show as a Cockney comic at 1 pm. He stayed 36 weeks. A part in radio's *Educating Archie* led to appearances in ITV's *Two's Company* with Libby Morris and *It's a Square World* with Michael Bentine, and on to his own series, *Emery at Large*. He was voted TV Entertainer of the Year and compered the Royal Variety Performance in 1972.

For years he owned and flew his own plane; he also enjoyed fast cars and motorcycles and had a portable gym. However, he was an insecure man: 'The thought of drying in front of an audience debilitates me to such an extent that I become sick with nerves,' he confessed. His private life was chaotic. He married five times – all his wives being showgirls – and left the last one to set up home with yet another showgirl 30 years younger than him. He died in 1983, aged 65.

Stanley Baxter

Stanley Baxter also played a range of characters of which the most popular were women. They included scullery maids, murderous grannies and even the Queen, but the most remarkable were impersonations of glamorous Hollywood stars such as Carmen Miranda, Alice Faye and the Andrews Sisters, in which he showed shapely legs.

He was born in Glasgow in 1928 and at seven entertained church elders with his imitation of Sir Harry Lauder. At 14 he was in plays on radio's Children's Hour. On Friday afternoons before the end of school Miss Patterson used to say: 'Let's have 20 minutes of entertainment from Stanley.' When performing he became another person, and his shyness and inadequacy disappeared.

For a time he was a Bevin boy in the mines, picking stones out of coal on a conveyor belt at the surface. Then in the army he got into Combined Services shows in Singapore. After the war he became a straight actor, spending three years with Glasgow Citizens' Theatre, but he had a disagreement with a producer, moved south to London in 1959 and switched to variety. A year later he was starring in his own TV series.

He played countless characters, singing and dancing, and his spectaculars set standards for other costume comics. In *Stanley Baxter's Picture Annual* (which included a sketch in which the Pope met the Godfather) he played 37 different characters requiring 37 wigs and 37 costume changes. His shows moved from BBC to ITV and back to the BBC, but they were enormously

costly both in money and time and the BBC called a halt to them in 1988, as a result of which Baxter became *Mr Majeika* in an ITV children's series about a defrocked wizard condemned to teaching at an English school after failing his wizardry exams.

'I was fed up with being fired,' he said. 'First it was the BBC, then LWT and then the BBC again. I know it was always because of the expense – it was an expensive show – but it brought them in BAFTA awards as well. When the BBC came back to me and said they were now ready to make another one-man show I was too busy doing *Mr Majeika*. Anyway, it was time I hung up my tights. More years of putting on

★ Stanley Baxter again, spoofing television as Mrs Bridges, the grumpy but warm-hearted cook played in *Upstairs Downstairs* by the late Hermione Baddeley ★

a leotard to do those glamorous ladies would have been really very tacky. People would have been saying, "Isn't he pushing his luck a bit here?" Maybe it was time to break off anyway.'

Larry Grayson

Larry Grayson, of course, does not dress up as a woman, although he used to do so. His first tour in drag was when he was 14; his hair was in a fringe and he wore a beret and a short frock and carried a sling handbag. His opening line was, 'I've just returned from Portsmouth.' Eventually he dispensed with the dresses and has since played a woman without dressing as one. He says he thinks of himself on stage as a middle-aged, Wincarnis-addicted woman with varicose veins.

He never really tells a joke. He gets laughs from the way he says things, with a lifted eyebrow, a shocked expression or an effeminate patting of his hair. Much of it is ad-libbed; he does not care for scripts. 'Oh dear, I've come over all giddy; I think it must be the brown bread,' he says. 'God, me hair needs washing, have you got a Kirby grip?'

His biggest fans are women over 40 who have been known to cry with laughter when he complains: 'My bones aren't half creaking today.' He says: 'Women laugh because it's like themselves.'

★ Playing a woman without dressing like one –
camp comedian Larry Grayson who says he thinks
of himself on stage as a middle-aged woman with
varicose veins ★

The framework of his act has been gossiping about a range of imaginary friends including Everard (a name he heard a Brighton landlady calling her 11-year-old son), Apricot Lil, who works in a jam factory, and Slack Alice, a coalman's daughter. 'Well, of course, Slack was very good at dancing in the early days, you know,' he says. 'I mean, her Black Bottom was never forgotten in Cleethorpes, and Everard was marvellous as well, especially with the Gay Gordons. Everard hates her and she hates him. It is mutual contempt. He used to go to the Cock and Trumpet until she started working behind the bar. Now he always uses the Friend in Hand, just down the road.'

Grayson says he got the style from landladies he has known. 'People wrote saying it was like a friend coming into the house because I just natter and chat.'

He was born Bill White in Banbury in the Twenties but his mother was deserted by his father when he was only nine weeks old and he was unofficially adopted by miner Jim Hammond, his wife Alice and their four daughters. Mrs Hammond died when he was six, after which the oldest girl, 'Our Fan', gave up her factory job to look after him. She also renounced her prospects of marriage. Her boyfriend told her to choose between him and the child. The boyfriend went.

Grayson was sickly. He suffered rheumatic feet and his legs were wrapped in cotton wool at night. He traded on his ill health and was spoiled. 'Ooh, Fan, I do feel poorly; I can't go to school,' he would say. Three hours later he would be in a cinema. He was fussy about clothes and has said that the reason he has never driven is that when other boys were going 'vroom-vroom' with toy cars he was pushing a doll's pram. He gave concerts in the wash-house at home, rigging up curtains, tap dancing and singing love songs, and charging a bottle top or a cigarette card for admission. At 14 he went to work in a local factory but left after a week. Then he worked in a shoe shop but quit after a day. Hammond said indulgently, 'Don't force him.' Soon he began entertaining twice weekly at a local working men's club under the stage name Billy Breen. He did two acts, wearing a white suit and singing *In the Bushes at the Bottom of the Garden* in the first half and getting into drag for the second.

A weak heart exempted him from military service but he entertained the troops. 'I'm terrified of the shelters,' he would tell them. 'Ooh the bombs.' They roared.

After the war, at his agent's suggestion, he changed his stage name from Billy Breen, taking his new surname from Kathryn Grayson, the Hollywood singing star, and then trying first names until he came to Larry. He also gave up drag and was a down-the-bill comic in summer shows and touring revues, at darts presentations and cricketers' dinners. He was resigned to never being a star but an appearance on *Saturday Variety* in 1972 led to a run of 10 shows from which developed a series, *Shut That Door!* The title came from his catch phrase, born at Brighton's Theatre Royal in 1970 when he felt a sudden draught while on stage and called the words into the wings.

He was voted Show Business Personality of the Year and invited to appear in a Royal Variety Performance. This led to *The Generation Game* in which he succeeded Bruce Forsyth as host and maintained its popularity with his own style. 'He seems like a nice boy,' he would say of a young male contestant, in the tone of a mother describing a daughter's boyfriend.

After deciding to leave *The Generation Game*, he did not appear on TV for four years until he presented the game show, *Sweethearts*. 'I've been offered lots of programmes but I didn't want to do something awful,' he explained. In the show he would interview three couples about how they met; only one was genuine. 'I never knew before the recordings which couple was genuine and I always got it wrong,' he said. 'The actors and actresses who play the other couples do it so well. I have been almost in tears at times – and then found out the story was all lies. The couple weren't lovers at all.'

He believes his camp comedy was before its time and he had to wait for a more liberal age to catch up with it, citing 'an old darling of 80' who thought he was called a camp comedian because he started at Butlin's. Gay rights activists have objected to his comedy. 'I can't think why they call themselves gay,' he says.

At home he is surrounded by memorabilia of stars he admired: 'my lovely Anna Neagle . . . lovely Jessie Matthews . . . my adored Gracie Fields'. He hand-waves and pirouettes much as on stage. At times he has talked of retiring and buying a little wool shop. One is never sure whether he is joking.

★

THE OUTRAGEOUS ONES

★

Some comedians shock – either with their material or their behaviour. Max Miller won a name for outrageousness with his blue jokes back in music hall days, but in recent years comedians have grown bolder, cracking jokes about subjects which were once taboo, and making headlines with their lives away from the studios. Here are four who have caused shock waves in the country.

Billy Connolly

Billy Connolly talks about 'willies' and sanitary towels, haemorrhoids and vomiting (or 'hewing and rolfing' as he calls it). He talks about tenement life, which he has defined as 'when there's 85 of you sharing the toilet and the seat's never cold'. His humour is raw, working class and macho. He distrusts flag-wavers and attacks bigotry and racism. His TV appearances are infrequent, largely because he will not accept cuts. 'I'm a comedian who gets warmed up as he goes along,' he says. 'I react to an audience. It takes all the energy out of a performance when they cut it about.'

He says he is not a television person anyway. 'I only go on talk shows to appear windswept and interesting. I don't like television, it's for dedicated non-thinkers. People say to me, "You could have a series." I would no more have a TV series than a nail through my forehead.'

Even on chat shows he makes an impact. He was a guest on one of Michael Parkinson's when the host was humiliated by Rod Hull's Emu and wound up on the floor, minus a shoe and his composure. Connolly showed that he was made of sterner stuff. When Emu turned to him he seized it by the throat and said: 'I'll tell you what, bird. You peck me and I'll break your neck and *his* bloody arm.'

As one of the presenters of the 1989 *Comic Relief* appeal show he flew to Mozambique to film his impressions of the state of the country and what needed doing. He thought it was an eminently suitable mission for a comic. 'The thing is to motivate someone to give dosh,' he said. 'The comedian standing in this unlikely place and saying unlikely things is a great motivator.'

The wild, giant Glaswegian, known as the Big Yin, was born in 1942. Like many Catholic schoolboys he wanted to be a priest and was clever at primary school, but then opted out. After leaving school he worked as a delivery boy for a Glasgow bookshop, and then for a baker before entering a five-year apprenticeship as a welder in the Clyde shipyards. At 23 he worked in Biafra on the building of an oilrig, made money and went to Jersey to work on a power station. He used to sing in the evenings and then decided to concentrate on his banjo. Back in Scotland he became a cult figure in the folk clubs among anti-apartheid and CND activists. Among the jokes he told then:

'A Glasgow sheriff asked a woman why she shot her husband with a bow and arrow. She said, "I didnae want tae wake the kids."'

'I don't think I'll ever get used to big rooms. When I was a kid the rooms were so small you could turn the light out and be in bed before it was dark.'

'Somebody once asked me how I slept at night. Just like a baby. I wake up every two hours crying and wetting myself.'

'A Scottish farmer was showing a Texan farmer round his wee place in Galloway. The Texan asks, "How big is this farm?" "Oh, just over eight acres." The Texan says, "Well, I have a farm back home and I can drive for two days and still be inside my own property." "Aye," says the farmer, "I used to have a car like that."'

'Ian Paisley's wife went to the dentist the other week. The dentist said, "How's the mouth?" She

★ Billy Connolly sending up heather-and-haggis
tartan kitsch and the commonly promoted image of
Scotland in *At Last It's Hogmanay*, a New Year's
Eve show for Channel 4 ★

said, "He's still in bed."'

He was merciless with hecklers. 'If my dog had a face like yours I'd shave its backside and make it walk backwards,' he would say.

With his marriage in trouble and drinking heavily, he moved south, becoming a star in England as well as Scotland, and fell in love with Australian comic Pamela Stephenson (see chapter 12). While his wife, Iris, was at home in Scotland with their two children, he was on the town punching paparazzi and swearing at reporters. 'I got blootered real easy,' he said later. 'It was because I was wholly unhappy.'

His billygoat beard and tangled hair caused him to be described as a walking midden and voted Britain's scruffiest man in 1983. Then he and Stephenson settled down. He had his hair trimmed and became a teetotal, non-smoking, vegetarian Buddhist. Michael Parkinson sent him a bottle of Perrier for his 43rd birthday with the message, 'For the man who's drunk everything.'

Connolly made new friends, including the Duke and Duchess of York, at whose wedding Connolly and Stephenson were guests – although their own two children were born without them marrying. 'Marriage is a wonderful invention, but so is a bicycle repair kit,' said Connolly.

He says he likes the new breed of comics though he rarely meets them. 'There's a thing I've always disliked and it was old people saying it. They used to say, "There are only seven basic jokes", and I used to think, "What crap!" And I love the way the boys have changed the direction of humour. Where religion and politics used to be taboo subjects, they are now the essential ingredients and racism is the taboo. I think I had a part in the changing of it because for a lot of years I was out there alone.'

Kenny Everett

Kenny Everett's career has been headlines all the way. He was sacked from his first job on pirate Radio London for sending up an advertiser, by Radio Luxembourg for confessing he smoked pot, and by the BBC for joking that a Transport Minister's wife passed her driving test by slipping the examiner a fiver. Capital Radio gave him a warning for saying 'piss off' on a programme.

At a Young Conservative meeting he called: 'Let's bomb Russia. Let's kick Michael Foot's

walking stick away.' The left branded him a fascist, though he explained: 'I only spoke because they asked me to. If Neil Kinnock had asked first I would have done his conference. I'm not political at all. I think all politicians should be rounded up and put in a blender.' Equalling matters up, he then outraged the right with a joke on radio about Margaret Thatcher. It was the sort of crudity sniggered at by schoolboys behind bike sheds and Radio Two showed him the red card for the second time.

'Welcome to my tacky little show,' he would say, introducing his television programmes. Nevertheless they acquired a following in all levels of society. The Princess of Wales reportedly told him: 'We always watch your show' when he was a guest at the 21st birthday party of her brother, Viscount Althorp, in 1985.

In the shows 'Kennypoo', as he referred to himself, played a range of comic characters, including Marcel Wave, a French hair stylist, Bruce Droop, an Australian beer guzzler, Captain Kremin, a space ace, Roger Mortis, an undertaker, Reg Prescott, an accident-prone do-it-yourselfer and, most famously, Cupid Stunt, a busty Hollywood starlet in fishnet tights. (A bizarre feature was that Everett retained his beard while playing her.) He was supported by the voluptuous Cleo Rocos and the Hot Gossip dance troupe whose costumes and routines set a new level of sexiness. Everett referred to them as 'the naughty bits' of his shows.

It was all, he liked to say, 'in the best possible taste'. He claimed: 'We never set out to shock people or be outrageous. People only say a joke is in bad taste if it doesn't make them laugh. If something's funny it's not offensive and vice versa.'

In 1985 fans were shocked by the revelation that he was homosexual. 'I suppose I'm gay because I was born with a little extra something in my genes,' he joked. 'By the way, you spell that J.E.A.N.S.' A Sunday newspaper broke the story just before he recorded his Christmas show. 'I was playing Queen Victoria in one sketch and I said to the audience, "The first one that calls me an old queen gets it." They fell about laughing. As long as you make them laugh they're fine.'

He said that at school he thought he had

★ Jasper Carrot, performing as usual with
the minimum of props ★

★ Full of plumptiousness in his diddy hat, Ken Dodd, the king of Knotty Ash and chronicler of its diddyfolk (above) ★

★ Gareth Hale and Norman Pace, who met at teacher training college (above); Tommy Cannon and Bobby Ball, who met while working as welders in a factory (right) ★

★ Bizarrely bespectacled, Dame Edna Everage (Barry Humphries) at the piano, decorated as usual with gladioli (left) ★

★ Stanley Baxter (above) doing a fair impersonation of Shirley Temple. ★

★ Versatile Bruce Forsyth, once the king
of light entertainment, but since 1980
seen mainly in game shows such as *Play
Your Cards Right* ★

★ 'Caviar butties all round!' decreed Liverpool's super-confident Jimmy Tarbuck when he became compere of *Sunday Night at the London Palladium* (right) ★

★ Bob Monkhouse hosting *Family Fortunes*, one of many game shows with which he has been associated (below) ★

★ Just like that! Tommy Cooper, the giant
with the expressive face and a repertoire of
magical tricks that went awry ★

★ 'And it's all in the best possible taste,' Kenny Everett liked to say ★

better start fancying girls only because the other boys did. Later he invented a girlfriend called Melanie Bubbles. When he married a pop singer and spiritualist medium seven years older than himself in 1967 it was because, 'I thought it would be so much easier to be straight. The sexual chemistry wasn't there but I hoped it would appear in time.' Although they parted after 11 years, Everett was best man when his ex-wife subsequently remarried.

Born Maurice Cole in Liverpool on Christmas Day 1944, he was a weedy boy in a school populated by dockers' sons. While still in short trousers he won a competition at the Liverpool Odeon for doing more rope skips than any other child – 280 of them. 'How stupid of me – skipping!' he says. 'Back at school I got beaten to death for it. And my dad – he used to drive a Liverpool tugboat, very heave-ho me hearties – he didn't go much on the

skipping either.'

Like Connolly he wanted to be a priest but according to his own account was thrown out of the seminary for helping himself to the holy wine and bread. At school he gravitated to a quiet spot in the playground, and he still avoids crowds. His pleasure was listening to radio and he learned to impersonate the Goons, buying two tape recorders with paper round earnings and making his own programmes. At 20 he started in pirate radio, and changed his name, taking 'Everett' from the American film comic Edward Everett Horton.

'Basically, darlings, I'm a shy and retiring person,' he says. 'I'll do anything for a camera, although I'm only daring in the safety of a TV studio. I'd still rather die than face a live audience and I never do stage shows or club appearances.'

Freddie Starr

Freddie Starr, another Liverpudlian, may not have inspired as many headlines as Everett but he was the subject of Fleet Street's most celebrated banner of recent years. It was in *The Sun* of 13 March 1986:

Freddie Starr Ate My Hamster

The story began: 'Zany comic Freddie Starr put a live hamster in a sandwich and **ATE** it, model girl Les La Salle claimed yesterday.' The model alleged that Starr was staying with her and her boyfriend, came in late one night and demanded a sandwich. 'Get it yourself,' she said, whereupon: 'He put my hamster between two slices of bread and started eating it.' The hamster's name was Supersonic.

Starr denied it from the start; the fact that it was published speaks for his reputation. He is widely regarded as a comic genius, but wild, difficult and unpredictable, though extravagantly generous to friends and acquaintances. He supposedly threw a gold Rolex watch worth £6,000 into the Thames, saying, 'Baubles mean nothing to me.' He insists: 'The reputation I've got is mostly bar talk; stories get exaggerated. I've changed – I changed my underpants only last week.' He then speaks of his loyalty to Queen and country in one breath and boasts of criminal friends in the next.

Born in 1944, a carpenter's son, he began entertaining by mimicking teachers at his secondary modern school. 'I was always getting the stick for it too,' he says. 'There was one who used to wear a bowler hat and carry a cane like Charlie Chaplin. When he left the room I used to put ink on my top lip, put on a hat and strut around like Chaplin.'

He was a bricklayer and a boxer before becoming nationally known as a comic as the hit of the 1969 Royal Variety Performance. On stage, frequently in Teddy Boy suit and crepe-soled shoes, he is a big draw. He impersonates Adolf Hitler and Max Wall, and Adolf Hitler impersonating Max Wall, though he is most admired for his Elvis Presley act. In the impressions show, *Who Do You Do?*, in the Seventies, he also appeared as Norman Wisdom, Mick Jagger and wrestler Adrian Street. In the United States in 1987 he impersonated Johnny Cash, John Wayne, Dean Martin, Gene Kelly and – pulling a black stocking over his head – Ray Charles. The talent is great but, rightly or wrongly, television executives are wary of him.

Joan Rivers

Joan Rivers has been called the funniest woman in America. She has also been called a walking version of the poison pen, and grating and tasteless. She made her reputation by ridiculing celebrities, particularly Elizabeth Taylor in her barrage balloon phase. Liz Taylor, she said at different times, 'has got more chins than a Chinese telephone directory.... She's so fat she wears stretch kaftans.... Mosquitoes see her and scream, "Buffet".... She's the only one I know who stands in front of the microwave shouting, "Hurry Hurry".... She pierced her ears and gravy ran out.' And much more like that.

Taylor, of course, subsequently shed her excess poundage. Rivers claimed credit. 'I'm the reason she got thin and she's grateful. Her men weren't telling her she was fat. I did her a great service.' It may be so. Rivers says Taylor sent flowers and telephoned solicitously when Rivers's husband, producer Edgar Rosenberg, was in hospital.

However, Rivers viewed the slimmed-down Taylor with concern. 'I'm furious, one more year as a fat pig and I'd have had a new house, but you can't joke about her when she's thin. I'm hoping she'll become anorexic because that will open up a whole new ball game.'

No one is safe from her whiplash tongue. Some of her comments on other celebrities were:

Bo Derek: 'The woman is an idiot. She turned down the role of Helen Keller; she couldn't remember the lines.'

Robert Mitchum: 'If he'd just wear deodorant. Standing downwind, Mitchum is probably the sexiest man going.'

Yoko Ono: 'You know how she got her name? John Lennon saw her naked and said, "Oh no." Yoko Ono is one of the reasons Ray Charles is glad he can't see.'

Jackie Onassis: 'Has eyes on either side of her head like ET.'

Christina Onassis: 'The ugliest woman in the world. First time I met her I thought she was wearing a fur coat – she was in a strapless dress.'

Madonna: 'So hairy that when she lifted up her arm I thought it was Tina Turner in her armpit.'

Tina Turner: 'She looks like she's been to the electric chair and lived.'

Joan Collins (when she was married to fourth husband Peter Holm, who was younger than her): 'She paid 50,000 dollars for her ticket to the Florida ball for Prince Charles and Princess Di; she got a child's ticket for her husband.'

Britain's royal family came in for their share of insults. 'The royal family are all dogs. The ugliest of all is Princess Anne. What a horse. Did you watch the wedding? (Prince Charles's) She ate the bridal bouquet.' Of the Princess of Wales: 'Princess Di wears more clothes in one day than Gandhi wore in his entire life.' Of Princess Michael of Kent: 'Like a tall Nazi.' Of the Queen: 'Gowns by Helen Keller.'

According to Rivers all public figures are fair game. 'I pick on the biggest. They can take it. I'll not pick on someone who can't defend himself. That's mean spiritedness. If I thought I was hurting anyone the line would come straight out.' She says Nancy Reagan asked her to lay off the Reagan children and she obliged.

In fairness, it must be said that she does not spare herself. She says that as a girl she was so fat she took up the entire front row in her school form photo. Three stage hands once saw her nude. 'One threw up, the others turned gay.' On the night of her wedding her husband said gently, 'Let me undo your buttons.' She was naked at the time. At 28 she was single and

★ 'Unfunny and crude' was how some viewers described Joan Rivers in letters to the BBC after her series, *Can We Talk?* ★

expensively gowned and enviably attractive. (She admits to having had an eyelid tuck and a nose job.)

She claims: 'Poking fun at stars is really only about 20 per cent of my act. The rest of it has to do with self-deprecating humour, and humour directed primarily at women. Women love my humour because I make sex silly, bawdy, funny and not dirty.' She talks about menstrual periods, housework, cheap airline flights, stewardesses, having babies by natural childbirth, and mean nurses. 'I know what I'm going to talk about, the areas,' she says, 'but I don't know how it's going to come out. It's like a deck of cards. You throw it up, you may catch this or that one.... Offstage I'm very methodical. I have every joke worked out and written down, then I cross-index and cross-file them.'

She was born Joan Molinsky in Brooklyn, New York, in the Thirties. Her father, a doctor, was an emigrant from Russia and she was privately schooled. In her early days as an actress she worked as an office temp, slept in her car and washed at a YWCA. Her first marriage to a clothing store heir lasted only six months. When she switched to comedy she worked in Greenwich Village clubs, seedy burlesque houses and strip joints. 'If a trash can had a light bulb in it I appeared there,' she says.

Her career took off in 1965 following an appearance on Johnny Carson's *The Tonight Show* (after being turned down seven times) and in 1983 she became the programme's regular stand-in host for eight weeks a year while Carson was on holiday. Ratings soared. However, after her BBC2 series, *Can We Talk?* in 1986, in which she asked page three girl Samantha Fox if she was a virgin and Bernard Manning if he really hated homosexuals, the BBC reported that correspondents called her unfunny and crude.

In 1987 she shocked a club audience in Los Angeles by making jokes about her husband Edgar, who had killed himself with a drink and drugs cocktail because of a heart disease. They had been married more than 20 years but reportedly she joked: 'I couldn't even identify my husband's body – I hadn't looked at it for years', and claimed she told the mortuary attendant: 'I think that looks like him. Let me see the ring.' Some of the audience booed. It is still possible to be too outrageous.

desperate. 'I'd get an obscene phone call and say "Hold on a minute – let me get a cigarette."' She once dated a transvestite. 'My mother said, "So marry him – you'll double your wardrobe."'

Other jokes against herself run: 'I nearly gave my husband a heart attack the other night; we were making love and I took the paper bag off my head.... My body is so bad a Peeping Tom looked in my window and pulled down the shade.' It is all absurd. She is 5 ft 2 in tall, slim,

SITCOM COMICS

★

Situation comedies make up the greatest part of televised comedy today and most of them are still – as they always have been – about frictions in family life. The pattern was set as early as 1951 when *I Love Lucy* began in America with Lucille Ball as Lucy Ricardo (née McGillicuddy), well-meaning and lovable, but scatterbrained and child-like.

Lucille Ball

I Love Lucy was the first American situation comedy seen in Britain; it began in ITV's opening week in 1955 as the highlight of Sunday night viewing, and Ball's picture was on the cover of the first issue of *TV Times*. Striving to be a supportive wife, while yearning for a career in show business, Lucy taxed the patience of her Cuban bandleader husband, Ricky, who was played by Ball's Cuban bandleader husband, Desi Arnaz. In the war of the sexes, Lucy was aided by neighbour Ethel Mertz (Vivian Vance); Ricky was supported by Ethel's husband Fred (William Frawley).

The series was the stars' own idea. They made a pilot and interested a network in it, but executives had reservations. They wanted to replace Arnaz with Richard Denning and to make the show in New York. The stars eventually won the battle, conceding cuts in salary but obtaining the rights to the 'residuals', the earnings of the shows after their first screening. This deal was to make them a fortune.

Typical episodes involved Lucy getting the idea Ricky was plotting to kill her, trying to be a pal to her husband by joining him in a poker game, attempting to lose 12 pounds in order to break into show business, getting on a quiz show, and dividing the living room in half in a bid to persuade Ricky to be tidy around the house.

In its first season *I Love Lucy* ran second in popularity to *The Red Skelton Show,* but then Ball became pregnant. Her pregnancy was written into the script, though network delicacy then required that she was referred to as 'expecting'. This happened in America on the night before President Eisenhower's inaugural address in 1953 and she got an audience of 44 million compared with Eisenhower's 29 million.

Ball delivered a boy, Desi Jr, who was written into the stories, and the Ricardos became an established part of American life. An estate agent in Connecticut, offering a furnished cottage to rent, chose as a selling point, 'a cocktail table that is a replica of the one in *I Love Lucy*'. The Marshall Field department store in Chicago began closing an hour earlier on Mondays so that customers and staff could get home in time to watch the show. A parent-teacher association in Lynn, Mass. demanded the local station screen the programme earlier so that children could be got to bed. A Lions Club in Santa Barbara, California bought a TV set and adjourned meetings for half an hour at programme time to draw members.

Lucille Ball, born in 1911 in Jamestown, New York, had always had to struggle – as a model, a salesgirl, a waitress, a bit-part player, a Goldwyn Girl and a radio comedienne. She had been in 70 movies, but became a superstar only at 40 when she turned to TV. On television she and her husband were in charge. They pioneered filming before a studio audience, ensuring preservation of the shows, to which, through their company, Desilu, they controlled distribution and rights. In a few years Desilu was a giant, owning the RKO studios where they had been under contract when making *Dance, Girl, Dance* in 1940.

It was while making that film that they met and decided to marry. Their marriage had struck rocks some years before *Lucy* started, and Ball had begun divorce proceedings, but they

★ Master Sergeant Ernie Bilko propounds another sure-fire money-making scheme to his men in *You'll Never Get Rich*, the series that established America's Phil Silvers as a never-to-be-forgotten star of television ★

★ Whatever schemes Dickie Henderson might have, he usually met his match in his TV wife (played by June Laverick). ★

★ For nearly a quarter of a century Lucille Ball was America's first lady of television comedy. *I Love Lucy* was a hit in almost every country of the world and made her one of the richest and most powerful stars in show business ★

were reconciled and had a second wedding in church. They claimed the series had solidified their marital happiness. When they had a row one would turn to the other and say, 'You know, this would make a perfect episode for *Lucy*', and they would start to discuss the script. Eventually this failed to work. In 1960, after 179 episodes of *I Love Lucy,* they were divorced and Arnaz sold his share of their company to Ball who later sold out to Paramount.

In 1961 she began 156 episodes of *The Lucy Show* as Lucy Carmichael, a widowed mother of two children, in Connecticut, followed in 1968 by the first of 144 episodes of *Here's Lucy* in which she played Lucille Carter, again a widow, but a secretary in California. Her children, Lucie Arnaz and Desi Arnaz Jr, appeared as Kim and Craig Carter, the children of her television character. *Here's Lucy* continued in production until Ball's retirement in 1974 at the age of 63. It was commonplace for there to be four or five showings of *Lucy* programmes on a single day in New York in the Seventies, and they were also being seen around the world. It was only in 1986 when she

returned to launch *Life with Lucy* at the age of 75 that her formula failed. She died in 1989.

Dickie Henderson

A curious feature of early sitcoms was that stars often played themselves, or television versions of themselves, using their own names. *The Dickie Henderson Show,* a British domestic sitcom of the Fifties, starred Henderson with June Laverick as his wife and ran to 120 episodes over 12 years.

The husky-voiced Henderson was born in London in 1922 and privately educated in Hollywood and England. His father, Dick Henderson Sr, was a celebrated comedian who was still turning cartwheels at 70, and his sisters Triss and Win had a song and dance act as the Henderson Twins. In Hollywood at seven, he

★ Apart from starring in his sitcom series, Dickie Henderson appeared frequently as a stand-up comic and song and dance man. He was an hilarious eccentric dancer and a talented acrobat in falling-down routines ★

service as an RASC officer, he went into revues and pantomimes, making his TV debut in 1953 in *Face the Music.* He went on to appear in eight Royal Variety shows.

In a profession in which many stars give to charities, Henderson was outstanding. With Variety Club colleagues he launched a fund to buy the first special coach to take polio victims to the seaside; there are now more than 3,250 of them. He also involved himself in organisations concerned with spastics, polio and cystic fibrosis, driving miles to take part in charity concerts and golf tournaments, though he dismissed his tireless efforts mendaciously with, 'Well, it's easier than sending a cheque.' His work was recognised with an OBE in 1977.

Ill with cancer, he continued joking. When Jimmy Tarbuck visited him after an operation Henderson told him: 'I'm looking much better today. Now you know how I looked yesterday.' He also joked: 'It could be worse; I might have Aids.' A few weeks later he was dead. Henderson had always hated smut and worshipped professionalism, and years before his death in 1985 he had said: 'When I go I hope people will say, "He was a pro."' He was a pro – and a gentleman.

Eric Sykes

An even longer-running British sitcom was *Sykes.* Eric Sykes and Hattie Jacques came together in it in 1959 after meeting in radio's *Educating Archie.* (She appeared in it and he scripted it.) *Sykes* ran for 21 years, hardly changing.

It all began with *Sykes and the Telephone,* which had a script by Johnny Speight about the traumas of getting a phone installed. Sykes and Jacques were originally cast in traditional husband and wife roles but Sykes thought this would be restricting and result in yet another series about matrimonial misunderstandings, so he said, 'Make her my sister.' After that he wrote the scripts himself. They reflected old-fashioned innocence in a hard world. Sykes and Jacques played an odd, middle-aged couple living in a never-never land untouched by

was enrolled by his mother in a dance school run by Rita Hayworth's father.

He made his film debut at 10 in *Cavalcade* while touring America with his father and was in line for *David Copperfield* but his father said Hollywood was no place for the boy, and the part went to Freddie Bartholomew. Henderson returned to Britain and at 16 made his theatre debut as an eccentric dancer, joining his sisters on a tour of Scottish resorts. After wartime major events, a world where one could go to football matches without fear, where Christmases were white and summer holidays were sunny, and no one meant harm. It was simple, enjoyable escapism.

Its comedy was universal and visual for, as a writer, Sykes concentrates on situations and attitudes rather than gags. He says a favourite idea concerns a tin of corned beef which no one can open, a failure which eventually brings down a government. 'I believe in telling a story,' he says. He ignored Jacques's size – which, as she said, took some ignoring – and treated her as feminine and kittenish.

In the mid-Sixties he called a halt, unhappy that the series was being used in a ratings war when the BBC pitted it against ITV's *Coronation Street,* but after six years a tax bill drove him back to it and he ended it only after Jacques died in 1980 at the age of 56.

Sykes was born in 1923 in Oldham, Lancs, where his father worked in a cotton mill. He remembers a mill strike in 1928 when neighbours brought food to prevent the family starving. His own first job was in a cotton mill, where he discovered that by putting an empty bucket on his head he could sound like Bing Crosby. He was sacked while singing *In the Blue of the Night.*

Since the early Fifties he has suffered chronic hearing problems, which originally affected his right ear, but later both ears, causing him to pull out of a Royal Variety Performance in the Sixties. However, he has continued to write and

★ Hattie Jacques and Eric Sykes had one of the longest partnerships in TV comedy, appearing as siblings in shows written by Sykes from 1959 until her death in 1980 ★

perform. In 1967 he had a big success with *The Plank*, a comedy film for television about two idiots with a length of timber, which he wrote, directed and appeared in, and in 1987 made a sequel, *Mr H is Late*, playing an undertaker trying to get a client to the church on time. Freddie Starr, Bob Todd, Henry McGee and Eli Woods played pallbearers, Terry Scott drove the hearse, Jimmy Edwards was a traffic warden, and Kathy Staff the widow.

'I like to think the whole family is able to sit down and have a laugh,' says Sykes. 'I think it is my upbringing. I was raised very strictly. My parents taught me never to lie and to believe in right and wrong.'

Phil Silvers

An early American sitcom which broke away from a domestic background was set in the army and called *You'll Never Get Rich* when it began in America in 1955. It is now better known by other titles under which it has been sold around the world: *Sgt Bilko* and *The Phil Silvers Show*. It began on BBC TV in Britain in 1957.

Silvers was born in 1912 in Brooklyn, the son of Russian Jews. He was a professional song and dance man at the age of 12, and went on into Hollywood and Broadway musicals. In 1954 he was invited to Washington to appear in a stage show for President Eisenhower and scored a triumph from the moment he looked out at the audience, which included the President, Vice President Nixon, members of the administration, senators and congressmen, and exclaimed: 'My God, who's minding the store?'

Three days later the CBS network asked him to star in a show to be written by Nat Hiken. The role was that of Master Sgt Ernest Bilko, a conman in charge of the transport pool at an army base in Kansas. Bilko was dedicated to the pursuit of money and manipulating the army

★ Nothing is certain in television comedy. After his huge success as Sgt Bilko, Phil Silvers was entitled to expect another hit when he moved on to play a factory foreman in *The New Phil Silvers Show* in 1963. But it was a short-lived disaster ★

★ Alfie Bass played the 'boots' and Bill Fraser the major domo of an old-fashioned

system to acquire it. 'My new squad! New blood!' gloated Silvers, rubbing his hands in the first episode, before offering the recruits deals on razor blades and chewing gum, and launching a contest to find the platoon sweetheart. 'Men, this is it. Get your hips fitted for Jaguars,' he would exult, eyes glinting behind his glasses, when he thought he had hit upon a foolproof moneymaking scheme. 'I knew it, he's sold us into slavery,' Pte Fender (Herbie Faye) would wail when the scheme went awry.

The lines were delivered at machine-gun pace. One episode, *The Court Martial,* acclaimed a classic satire on bureaucracy, was about a chimpanzee inducted into the army. The chimp was standing in line with its owner and was accidentally enlisted as Private Harry Speakup, after which the only way to discharge it was to court martial it. Bilko was assigned as its defence counsel. At one point in the filming the chimp spotted a telephone on the set and picked it up. 'I plead for an adjournment,' Silvers ad-libbed to the actor playing the president of the court martial. 'My client is calling for a new attorney.'

For its first three years the show was filmed with three cameras before a New York audience, then to save time it was filmed in an empty studio and screened before an audience of GIs whose laughter was recorded and dubbed. There were 138 episodes over four years, but the series was expensive, involving a regular cast of 22, and the network ended it in 1959 with Bilko behind bars.

The New Phil Silvers Show in 1963, in which he was cast as a similarly avaricious factory foreman, was a flop. 'On the new series I had complete control, 100 per cent ownership,' said Silvers later, 'but after a few weeks it was clear I was the 100 per cent owner of a sinking ship.'

He developed a cataract on his left eye and drifted into emotional and financial depression. He and his wife parted and he sought psychiatric help. Nevertheless, he made some films and in 1972 won a Tony theatre award in *A Funny Thing Happened on the Way to the Forum.* Then he had a stroke and the show closed. Yet when he died in 1985 the original series was still being repeated in Britain and elsewhere.

Bill Fraser and Alfie Bass

ITV's first really big hit comedy series also concerned the military. *The Army Game* in 1957 was set in Hut 29 of Nether Hopping army camp. The cast included Michael Medwin,

club in London's West End in ITV's *Bootsie and Snudge*, a sequel to *The Army Game* ★

Harry Fowler, Dick Emery, Norman Rossington and Bernard Bresslaw, but the two favourite characters were diminutive Private 'Excused Boots' Bisley, played by Alfie Bass, and beady-eyed Sgt Major Claude Snudge played by Bill Fraser. The sergeant-major's 'Ave no fear, Snudge is 'ere,' and 'I'll be leaving you now, sah', became catch phrases.

Fraser and Bass were named top ITV Personalities of 1960 and given their own series, *Bootsie and Snudge,* in which they played the same characters after demobilisation as 'boots' and major domo in a gentlemen's club in St James's. They went on to play the roles more than 200 times though by 1963 they felt the characters were played out. 'The writers were running out of situations; there was a danger too we had become firmly typecast,' said Bass. So they went back to the theatre, Bass taking over Topol's lead role in *Fiddler on the Roof* for 600 performances in London's West End.

But viewers wanted more of Bootsie and Snudge and the characters were revived for a further series in the mid-Seventies with the formula that Bootsie had become the world's first £1 million pools winner and Snudge had given up a job with the pools firm to help him spend it. Their roles had been reversed; Bootsie

had become the dominant one and it was Snudge's turn to creep.

Bass was a small East Ender, born in Bethnal Green in 1921, the youngest of 10 children of a cabinet maker who had fled from Jewish persecution in Russia. Bass began amateur acting in boys' clubs – playing Lady Macbeth at the age of 12 – when he was not running the streets and being chased by police. He left school at 14 and was a tailor's apprentice, a messenger boy and a shopwindow display fitter before becoming a professional actor.

Fraser, a Scot, started out as a bank clerk in Perth before going on the stage. When roles were few he slept on the London Embankment, but later set up his own rep company in Worthing. 'I play stuffy, pot-bellied, pompous old sods,' he said. 'Thank God, England is full of them.' A critic once likened his voice to being 'funnelled through vintage port'. In fact, he kept a bottle of port in his dressing room and poured some when we talked in London's Whitehall Theatre in 1986. However, he claimed, 'My secret of youth is a daily dose of cod liver oil tablets washed down with a good Scotch.'

Bass died in 1987 aged 66. Fraser survived him by only a few weeks. He died at 79.

MADE BY RADIO

★

The first postwar television comics came from the theatre or radio, but mostly from radio, because they were accustomed to mastering a new script for each performance whereas music hall performers were worried about using up the material that was their stock in trade. Some of the earliest TV comedy shows were simply illustrated radio, a development that began in America.

George Burns

The George Burns and Gracie Allen Show, which transferred from radio to TV in America in 1950, was close to situation comedy with Burns playing himself, and Allen (his partner in vaudeville and radio since 1923 and his wife since 1926) playing herself. Their son Ronny played their stage son, and Bea Benaderet and Hal March were seen as their neighbours.

Where it differed from sitcom was that Burns would speak asides directly to viewers, and he and Allen retained the traditional vaudeville style of delivery. Allen would say something, Burns would repeat it, and then she would answer and get her laugh. Burns made a joke of this. 'From force of habit I repeat everything,' he said. 'I've been a straight man for so many years that when I went fishing with a fellow one day and he fell overboard and yelled "Help!" I said "Help!" While I waited for him to get his laugh he drowned.'

He and Allen also retained their traditional sign-off.

Burns: 'Say good night, Gracie.'
Allen: 'Goodnight Gracie.'

The first 50 of their TV shows were live. If a show was over-running the producer held up a sign saying 'Talk Faster'. If it was under-running they had to speak more slowly. For example, Burns was supposed to ask Gracie, 'Why did you put *two* roasts in the oven?' The producer held up the 'Talk Slower' sign and

Burns began to waffle: 'Gracie, let me ask you something, not that I'm inquisitive . . . and I know I shouldn't ask you this . . . but if I didn't ask you this I couldn't sleep . . . not that it's important . . . but there's something I'd like to know . . .' By this time the producer was holding up the 'Talk Faster' board and Burns had to spit out the question, and Allen had to gabble the punch line: 'When the little roast burns, the big one is done.'

After two years the shows were filmed and they continued until Allen retired in 1958, after which Burns continued alone for two years in *The George Burns Show.*

He was born Nathan Birnbaum in 1896, one of a family of seven sisters and five brothers whose parents came from Eastern Europe. His father pressed trousers in a sweatshop and they lived in a tenement on New York's East Side, with toilets in the yard. They had no radio and could not afford to go to the movies. Swimming in the East River was the main recreation of youngsters, but at seven Burns was a singer in the Peewee Quartet, and he was a small-time vaudeville artist when he married Gracie, whose own act was an Irish jig.

Allen died in 1964, a decade before Burns became a big star again at the age of 80 in the films *The Sunshine Boys* and *Oh God.*

Jack Benny

Burns was followed from radio to television within weeks by his rival, Jack Benny, a master of deadpan delivery who could stand motionless, saying nothing for seemingly minutes at a time. 'It's sheer gall,' he said. 'I sometimes

★ 'Hello playmates!' Big Hearted Arthur Askey on radio in 1949, four years before his first television series. The little man was one of the first of many comedy stars who have come from Liverpool ★

wonder how I have the nerve.' Actually, it was superb timing.

In *The Jack Benny Program* he and Mary Livingstone, his wife, played themselves. Others in the shows included Irish tenor Dennis Day, Eddie Anderson as Benny's black valet, Rochester, Frank Nelson as a shop assistant encountered in every shop Benny entered, and Mel Blanc as Benny's violin teacher, Professor Le Blanc. There were a number of recurring jokes in the shows which the BBC began screening in Britain in 1956. One was Benny's age. He was 56 when the shows began but professionally he was 39 and remained so. Another was Benny's meanness. He was reputed to keep his cash in a vault and when told, 'You can't take it with you,' he retorted, 'In that case I'm not going to go.' In one sketch

★ 'Your money or your life,' demanded a hold-up man of Jack Benny. 'Come on, come on, hurry it up!' Replied Benny: 'I'm thinking it over.' His pretended meanness was one of the regular elements in Benny's comedy on radio and later on television ★

Rochester accepted a cable from a messenger boy in Benny's dressing room and having no small change to tip the boy, took a coin from Benny's trousers which were on a hook. Benny returned, picked up his trousers, weighed them in his hands and demanded, 'Who's had a quarter out of here?'

A third regular joke was Benny's violin playing. He used to walk on stage carrying a violin and declare: 'This is a genuine Strad. If you look inside you can see where it says so, right there. It says "Genuine Strad", then it is signed Antonio Stradivari, and then it gives the area code.' In fact, he did own a genuine Strad which he played with symphony orchestras for charity, despite a much-quoted newspaper review which read: 'Last night Jack Benny played Mendelssohn, and Mendelssohn lost.'

He was born Benjamin Kubelsky in Waukegan, Illinois, in 1894 and teamed as a violinist with a woman pianist before World War One. During the war the Navy put him in a variety show, gradually giving him more lines and reducing his violin playing until his fiddle was merely a prop. His radio series began in the early Thirties, and his TV series ran until 1965, by which time he was over 70, though still claiming to be 39. He died in 1974.

Arthur Askey

In Britain Arthur Askey had also made his name on radio before World War Two. In *Band Waggon* in 1938 the diminutive, Liverpudlian Askey was teamed with tall, Cambridge-educated Richard Murdoch. The plot had them living in a flat above Broadcasting House and keeping a goat named Lewis on the roof to save having to go down 49 steps and seven flights in a lift to fetch the milk. The series established the nicknames 'Big Hearted Arthur' for Askey and 'Stinker' for Murdoch, and also Askey's catch phrases, 'Hello playmates', and, 'I thank you' (pronounced 'Aythangyow'), which Askey acquired from London bus conductors.

His first TV series in 1953 was *Before Your Very Eyes,* a title chosen to emphasise that it was live. Each half hour show included three sketches with Askey playing such roles as Florence Nightingale, Sherlock Holmes and Rupert of Hentzau. The series was on BBC for four years, then on ITV for another four, before returning to the BBC. It was Askey who introduced Sabrina, a dumb blonde who did not act, sing, dance or speak. A former waitress named Norma Sykes, she simply breathed deeply and the male population did likewise for she had a 39-inch bust. At least, it was 39 inches when she first appeared; later she announced it had grown to 42 inches and she acquired a car with the registration S42. Askey swore he had not realised the size of her bust until a studio wardrobe mistress complained she could not get the girl into a medieval costume. All the

★ 'People think that all I do is stand up and tell a few jokes,' says George Burns. 'The jokes are easy. It's the standing up that's hard.' Rarely seen without a cigar, Burns was one of American television's first comics and was rediscovered for films at the age of 80 ★

publicity for the series soon centred on Sabrina rather than Askey and he decided the joke was over. 'She had to go,' he told me. She married an American doctor and went to live in Hollywood.

Askey was born in 1900 in Liverpool's dockland, the son of a book-keeper, and developed an ambition for show business while watching the Jovial Jesters, a pierrot troupe, on the sands during the family's annual two weeks holiday at Rhyl in North Wales. He first

★ Two more faces of Arthur Askey, who went on singing and clowning until his death in 1982. Ernie Wise said of him, 'I'm half of a double act; Arthur is half of a single act.' ★

realised the ambition when he was called up in World War One and began to entertain at army shows. After his demob he joined concert parties on the circuit of seaside resorts.

When he celebrated 50 years in show business in 1974 all the comedy stars attended a Variety Club lunch to pay tribute to him. Max Bygraves said: 'He's been in every comedy show except *Crossroads* and he only failed that because he was word perfect.' Eric Morecambe joked: 'Arthur went to see Lew Grade the other day. He was dressed in his brown suit, with brown shoes and a brown shirt and tie. When Lew saw him he picked him up, put him in his mouth and lit him.'

Askey was then a septuagenarian and had suffered a heart attack seven years earlier. When he met Prince Charles the Prince asked, 'Are you still working?' Askey said, 'But of course.' The Prince laughed: 'I suppose you're one of those fellows who'll probably die in harness.' Askey said later, 'I hope he's right.' He was. The little man worked until his death in 1982.

Jimmy Edwards

Bluff, hectoring, obstreperous, and with 'wizard prang' handlebar moustaches, Jimmy Edwards was a star of radio's *Take It From Here* in 1948 with Australia's Dick Bentley and Joy Nichols. His first TV series was *Whacko!* for the BBC in 1956 as the blustering headmaster of Chislebury School, a role which reflected his stage act in a mortarboard as 'Professor' Edwards, bellowing, 'Wake up at the back, there.' The series was, he said, 'Traditional English kind of humour which comes right from *The Magnet* and Billy Bunter.' A running gag was when he would say, 'I must gain some refreshment from the arts,' and take down a volume of Shakespeare containing a bottle of whisky. 'I am, in fact, what you would call a steady drinker,' admitted Edwards.

He also starred in the Seventies in *The Glums,* the television version of a domestic sitcom which was originally a segment of *Take It From Here* in 1950. Edwards played boorish, loud-mouthed Mr Glum, always seeking another brown ale, Dick Bentley was his dim son, Ron, and June Whitfield played the part of Ron's fiancée, Eth.

James Keith O'Neill Edwards, whose father actually was a professor, was born at Barnes in 1920 and educated at St Paul's Cathedral Choir

★ 'Wake up at the back,' roared Jimmy Edwards in his act as a bullying schoolmaster. The luxuriant 'wizard prang' handlebar moustaches were a legacy of his days as a Dakota pilot in World War Two when he won the DFC ★

School. As head boy he carried the cross at a service celebrating King George V's Silver Jubilee in 1935, and a singer's scholarship took him to St John's College, Cambridge to gain his MA. In World War Two he became Flight Lieutenant Edwards, a Dakota pilot, and towed a glider packed with paratroops to Arnhem. On the way back from a later supply trip to Arnhem he was caught by a Focke-Wulfe, and though he took evasive action the German plane got on his tail and its guns raked the wings and fuselage of the Dakota, which lost hydraulic oil and power. Edwards had to crash-land, suffering burns, but was back in the air six months later in another Dak and was awarded the DFC.

Leaving the RAF in 1946 with £98 and a demob suit, he decided to be a comic on the strength of appearances in *Footlights* revues at Cambridge and concerts in the RAF, and opened at London's Windmill Theatre in 1946 in his schoolmaster role and playing a euphonium.

Although born in a semi-detached, he adopted the style of a country squire, owning a 900-acre dairy farm in Sussex with 300 cows, hunting and playing polo, piloting himself to

matches in his own aircraft. He also stood unsuccessfully for parliament as a Conservative in 1964. A homosexual, he was married and divorced.

In 1958 when installed as first rector of St Luke's College, Exeter, he said: 'I cannot think why all the best brains of our country should have devoted their time to inventing television. It means that we are becoming a nation of short-sighted, hunch-backed troglodytes. The only good thing about it is that it presents a means for employment for me.' No one was sure whether he was serious. He died in 1988 aged 68.

★ Max Bygraves has made a speciality of nostalgia, featuring songs of bygone years. Some of his jokes are golden oldies too. ★

Max Bygraves

Max Bygraves made his name in radio's *Educating Archie,* which starred ventriloquist Peter Brough and his dummy, Archie Andrews, in 1950. He played an odd job man and introduced the catch phrases: 'A good idea – son', 'I've arrived and to prove it I'm 'ere', and 'big 'ead'.

He is now a millionaire, and has joked to audiences: 'I don't mean to be big about this but at 35 I had a house in London, a house in the country, three of the loveliest kids, an adorable wife. I had a few quid in the bank, all my tax was paid up to date and I was riding around in a Rolls-Royce. But do you think I was happy. Do you? You're bloody right I was.'

He has a clifftop house in Bournemouth with a swimming pool – for washing his money in, according to Jimmy Tarbuck. He also has flats in London and in Australia where he spends some months every winter, telling audiences: 'It's the British government's idea; they're going to keep sending me here until you take back Rolf Harris.' He maintains: 'The public don't begrudge you so long as you're not flash and you don't go scooting off looking for a tax-free haven abroad.'

He owes his wealth both to his jokes, delivered in a relaxed and confident manner, and his records of which he has sold 40 million singles and seven million albums. They began with *Cowpuncher's Cantata* (a medley of *Riders in the Sky, Mule Train* and *Jezebel)* in 1952, followed by *Heart of My Heart, Gilly Gilly Ossenfeffer Katzenellen Bogen by the Sea, Meet Me on the Corner, You Need Hands* and *Tulips from Amsterdam.*

His later 'singalong' records started when his mother complained there was no music around she liked. He made the first record for her, and went on to record 600 songs in five years. Sales were aided by TV series under such titles as *Singalongamax* and *Lingalongamax.*

A story which may or may not be true concerns a thief who stole a tape recorder and some tapes from a hotel at Hayling Island but sent them back with a note saying: 'Now I've sobered up I'm sorry. You can have them back. Besides, I hate Max Bygraves.'

In a long career in which he has remained remarkably youthful-looking, he has perhaps been less than successful only once, and that was as host of the quiz show *Family Fortunes.* Viewers compared him unfavourably with Bob Monkhouse, whom he had succeeded.

He was born in 1922 in Rotherhithe, London, where his father was a casual dock labourer and boxer, and nine members of the family lived in a two-bedroom flat. Bygraves shared a bed with his brother and grandfather; there was another bed in the same room for his four sisters. As a boy he dredged wood from the Thames and sold it for a penny a bucket. He was nine before he saw a chicken or a cow.

He worked as a carpenter in Lewisham before he enlisted in the RAF to become an air-frame fitter, working on Spitfires during the Battle of Britain. In a NAAFI canteen LAC Bygraves responded to an appeal for volunteers to do a turn and impersonated Max Miller, which is how the man christened Walter Bygraves came to be called Max. More than a thousand camp concerts gave him the experience which has since led to 18 Royal Command Performances.

Tony Hancock

Tony Hancock was another graduate of *Educating Archie,* and went on to become the favourite TV comic of his time. He was born in 1924 in Birmingham but when he was three the family moved to Bournemouth where his father took a hotel. His father was a semi-pro entertainer who wore a collapsible top hat and a monocle on stage. Hancock said: 'I don't think they like him very much actually, but that's understandable because his first joke was "Put the Rolls in the garage, Harvey, and don't forget to butter them."'

Variety artists who visited the hotel included Clapham and Dwyer, Elsie and Doris Waters, Stainless Stephen and the Houston Sisters, and Hancock gravitated naturally towards the stage. In the early days of the war he dressed like Max Miller with a hat on the back of his head and white and tan shoes, and was billed as 'Anthony Hancock, the Confidential Comic'. In 1942 he was called up into the RAF Regiment, auditioned for ENSA but dried completely after 'Ladies and Gentlemen'. However, Squadron Ldr Ralph Reader accepted him for a forces *Gang Show* and Hancock spent the rest of the war entertaining the troops in North Africa, Italy, Malta, Yugoslavia, Greece, Crete and Gibraltar.

After his demob in 1946 he claimed he lived on a sausage a day until his first job in another

★ Tony Hancock first became known as a star in the radio series *Educating Archie*. He was seen as a coffee bar employee on ITV in the Sixties, but will be best remembered for his sketches for the BBC, such as *The Blood Donor* (right) in which he confronted a nurse played by June Whitfield ★

Ralph Reader Gang Show called *Wings,* which had a cast of 300 ex-RAF men. Then he went to the Windmill Theatre in a double act with pianist Derek Scott during which Hancock did impressions of the famous, including George Arliss, the British film actor of the Thirties. This was an idea he got from a friend of his father's, a Bournemouth postman, who had impersonated Arliss when Hancock was a boy.

In a summer season at Bognor Regis he added Robert Newton as Long John Silver, Charles Laughton as the hunchback of Notre Dame and Captain Bligh of the Bounty; he also impersonated the town crier, athletes and the diving swimmer seen in the opening of the Gaumont-British cinema news.

In 1951 he succeeded Robert Moreton as tutor to Archie Andrews with the catch phrase, 'Flippin' kids'. His own series, *Hancock's Half Hour* followed on radio in 1954 with regulars Sid James, Bill Kerr and Kenneth Williams and later Hattie Jacques. By 1955 the character of Anthony Aloysius St John Hancock of 23 Railway Cuttings, East Cheam, was established, along with such catch phrases as 'Stone me' and 'You buffoon'. The character was pompous, arrogant, petty, ignorant and argumentative – yet sympathetic.

Hancock transferred to TV in 1956, adopting a homburg hat and a coat with an astrakhan collar. As a juryman in an episode titled *Twelve Angry Men* he demanded: 'Does Magna Carta mean nothing to you? Did she die in vain?' Other classic sketches included *The*

Blood Donor and one about a boring Sunday afternoon in which much of the dialogue consisted of weary sighs.

By 1960 the show commanded audiences of 12 to 13 million, but Hancock was discontented and not easy to work with. Bill Kerr had been dropped when the show moved to TV. Kenneth Williams quit soon afterwards. Hattie Jacques was used only occasionally. In 1960 Hancock parted company with Sid James, losing the perfect foil; he reasoned that his scope was reduced because a part always had to be written for James. Finally he split with his brilliant writers Ray Galton and Alan Simpson, and *Hancock's Half Hour* came to an end. His ambitions centred on films, but he failed to equal his television success.

'I've been criticised quite a lot because I try to move on, and the British public, though very loyal in many ways, are very resilient to change,' said Hancock on ITV's *The Frost Programme* in 1967. 'But comedy is such a fascinating art that you cannot stay static and just collect the cheque. It's very good for the bank but after a time you must experiment to a certain extent, and I think people resent this until they get used to your new way of presenting comedy.'

He failed to find the new way, drank heavily and killed himself in Australia in 1968. The public felt a great sense of loss, and have gone on watching re-runs and buying videos of his *Half Hours*.

Spike Milligan

To many comics Spike Milligan is a genius of comedy, whose anarchic *The Goon Show* on radio inspired many television series including *Monty Python's Flying Circus*. It grew out of a meeting between Milligan and Harry Secombe when they were both lance-bombardiers in the army during the campaign in Tunisia. Milligan fired a howitzer, insecurely based on rocks, and the recoil hurled it off, narrowly missing Secombe. Later they were both in army entertainments. (Milligan's pre-war ambition was to be a jazz trumpeter.) When they met again after the war Secombe, who was in radio's *Educating Archie*, introduced him to Peter Sellers and Michael Bentine and they found they shared the same lunatic sense of humour.

Over coffee and fish and chips they dreamed up the Goons, though the original title was *Crazy People*. Milligan undertook to write it, and it began in 1951, with Secombe playing the central character, Neddie Seagoon, and Sellers, Bentine and Milligan providing the voices of most of the other characters such as Bluebottle, Major Denis Bloodnok, Capt. Hercules Grytpype-Thinne, Minnie Bannister and Henry Crun. It was packed with lines that became catch phrases: 'It's all in the mind, you know.... You silly twisted boy.... Needle, nardle, noo.... I've been sponned.... Only in the mating season.... Damn clever, these Chinese.... You can't get the wood, you know.'

Secombe says: 'We didn't realise it but into humour had come a new sort of anarchy, a crazy intellectual comedy. *The Goon Show* was a kind of aural cartoon.' However, it was not an immediate hit. Secombe says: 'At first it had a rating of .001. There's a report of one BBC meeting where an executive said, "Now about this blasted Go On Show, ..." But eventually it acquired cult status.

By the time it ended in 1958 Milligan had already moved into TV with *The Idiot Weekly, Price 2d* with Sellers, Valentine Dyall, Graham Stark and June Whitfield, and this was followed by *A Show Called Fred* and *Son of Fred*. Milligan has continued writing and performing in series including *Milligan's Wake* and *Q5* and its successors which introduced such lines as, 'There's a cheque in the post', and 'There's a lot of it about.'

However, Milligan paid a heavy price for the intensity of his work on the Goons. 'It broke up my marriage and put me in a mental home five or six times,' he says. 'I've never got over the effects of it.' His first breakdown and hospitalisation was in 1956, though it did not impair his sense of humour. 'One day I tried to get all the lunatics to break the world record for getting people in a toilet,' he says. 'We got about 18 of us into one WC and they couldn't get us out. The local firemen came and opened the door, and one of the patients said, "If you come in, I'll pull the chain."' His tombstone, he says, will proclaim: 'I told you I was ill.'

He has long been a favourite of members of the royal family and on the Queen's birthday in 1965 Princess Margaret took her, Prince Philip,

★ Spike Milligan, a tireless campaigner for animal welfare and preservation of the environment, eats a cake in the shape of the Natural History Museum during one of his protests in 1982. Milligan makes people laugh – but is not a happy man ★

Prince Charles, Princess Anne and Peter Sellers to a theatre to see Milligan in *Son of Oblomov*. 'Why does Prince Philip wear red, white and blue braces?' shouted Milligan from the stage. Sellers called back from the audience: 'I don't know. Why does Prince Philip wear red, white and blue braces?' and Milligan delivered the punch line, 'To keep his trousers up.' Some claimed the Queen was not amused, but Sellers and Milligan later joined the royals for dinner at the Palace.

Milligan has never been predictable. As a guest on a live television discussion programme on comedy hosted by Wolf Mankowitz in the Fifties he leapt from his chair as the opening music started and, with 15 seconds to go, ran behind a cameraman and bit his ear. The titles faded to sounds of laughter and the sight of Milligan walking back to his chair, tucking his shirt into his trousers and doing up the fly.

He was born Terence Alan Milligan in Ahmaddnagar, India, in 1918 when his father was an NCO in the Indian army. Both his parents entertained at troop concerts. He came to England when he was 14, when the army made his father redundant. His humour has extended beyond radio and TV into many books including memoirs, limericks and abstract nonsense, and his *Ying Tong Song* has been a best-selling record. Yet Milligan is not a happy man. He is angered by inhumanity in the world and his own inability to combat stupidity, ignorance and indifference. 'I can't stand injustice,' he says.

Child abuse moves him to tears. 'There is only one truly barbaric animal on earth and that is man; the human race is not a very nice species,' he argues. He also rails against bureaucrats, hooligans, smoking and piped pop music. He sends letters to world leaders and to newspapers. He backs Greenpeace, Friends of the Earth and the World Wildlife Fund. 'I support all the causes that are trying to increase the sensitivity of the human race to the odious things that they do,' he says.

One labour of love from which he derived pleasure was restoring the Elfin Oak, a wood sculpture in Kensington Gardens. In 1898 a sculptor had carved the stump of a once mighty oak, destroyed by lightning, with about 70 tiny pixies, fairies and elves, and 150 forest creatures, toads, rabbits and woodpeckers. In 1962 Milligan obtained Ministry of Works permission to restore it – free of charge. During the four years he spent on the work a newspaper reporter tracked him down at the tree where he was remodelling lost limbs and asked, 'What is it about this tree that you like so much?'

Milligan glowered. 'I love it,' he said, 'because I don't have to make it laugh.'

Michael Bentine

Peter Sellers, of course, went on to become an international star in comedy films. He died in 1980. Michael Bentine devised innovative TV comedy, notably in *It's a Square World* and *All Square* in the Sixties. These series used animated table-top models and diagrams, and trick photography, and one memorable scene showed a Chinese junk sailing up the Thames and attacking the Houses of Parliament.

Bentine was born in Watford in 1922, his father a Peruvian who came to England in 1900. Bentine, an old Etonian, served in RAF Intelligence, working with Polish squadrons during the war, before developing a comedy act

★ Michael Bentine, 'the Peruvian from Watford', responsible for some innovative series ★

71

with a chair back, which he used to represent almost anything from a submarine periscope to a harp.

In 1972 he suffered the first of several tragedies when his eldest son, Gus, was killed when a small aircraft in which he was flying crashed in the New Forest. It took nine weeks for his body to be found. Bentine did not work for a long time – until friends suggested he should develop an idea he had for children's characters. They became *The Potties,* featureless puppets on which could be imposed wigs and moustaches. Bentine declared: 'People are within, not without. A Potty is a character who

★ *The Potties* were puppets created by Michael Bentine for an ITV children's series in the Seventies when he returned to work after the tragic death of his son ★

can change his nature with the help of the costume or design department. He is neither black nor white, Jew nor Christian, hippy nor bureaucrat, but he can be transformed into anything at the whim of the programme.'

Then his daughter Elaine died of cancer in 1983, and another daughter, Fusty, of the same cause in 1987. His wide interests in the paranormal and supernatural, which began when he was a boy, have since deepened and his television appearances have been infrequent.

Harry Secombe

In contrast with his ex-colleagues and many other comics, Harry Secombe is a man who seems always to be happy. Most reckon him to be Britain's happiest laughtermaker, forever pulling faces or blowing raspberries – the latter, he says, a habit which stemmed from

appearances at the Windmill Theatre in non-stop revue, six shows a day, six days a week, in 1946. If his jokes did not go well he blew a raspberry out of sheer fear. 'It was a nervous thing and that's how my funny noises began,' he says.

He laughs about almost anything. When he did an act in his early years, impersonating people shaving, and was fired by a manager in Bolton who told him, 'You'll shave in your own blank time,' he sent a telegram to Bentine: 'Audience with me all the way. Managed to shake them off at the station.' When he starred at the London Palladium for the first time in 1956 after breaking an arm on holiday, he joked: 'It's always been my ambition to play the Palladium with a huge supporting cast,' and pointed to the plaster.

He was born in Swansea in 1921, the son of a commercial traveller, and as a boy entertained at church socials with impressions of Sandy Powell, Stanley Holloway and Stainless Stephen. 'My very first concert,' he says, 'was at the Christmas social at St Thomas's Church and I was billed to do a Sandy Powell monologue, but when the curtains opened I just stood on the stage and stared. I couldn't find a word to say.'

He left school at 15 and was a junior pay clerk in a steel works before seven years in the army in North Africa, Sicily and Italy, ending in the central pool of artists. By the Fifties he had his own TV series, in which he sometimes used his fine voice to sing seriously, though more often, in his own words, he was 'mucking about' with songs. He used to sing the Nelson Eddy and Jeanette MacDonald duet, *Sweethearts*, taking both parts. Later he sang in the stage musical, *Pickwick,* and more recently in the Sunday ITV series, *Highway.* Since 1983 his television appearances have been mainly in *Highway,* which is shown in the religious slot, presenting and singing in more than 200 editions and travelling 100,000 miles in the course of the programmes. 'At first I wasn't sure I was the right man for the job because I was associated with frenetic comedy, but now I'm keen to do the show as long as they want me,' he says. He has written a novel, *Twice Brightly,* the story of a comic's first week in the theatre, and also collections of short stories under the titles *Goon for Lunch* and *Goon Abroad.*

He has shed much weight, which at one time

★ Rarely serious for long, comic knight Sir Harry Secombe clowns in nautical rig on a Thames pleasure boat during a Press junket to promote television programmes ★

reached more than 19 stone, since he was diagnosed as diabetic in 1979. Initially he took tablets but did not keep to his diet until in 1983 he nearly collapsed during a concert in Australia and was given two years to live if he did not adhere to it strictly. He then lost 5 stone.

He was knighted in 1981, whereupon Spike Milligan sent him a message: 'Someone has blundered.' He was even more amused when a Hong Kong customs officer addressed him as 'Mr Nowsir,' because his passport had been amended to read 'Now Sir Harry'. The knight of comedy giggles happily at the memory.

OUT OF UNIFORM

Like Max Bygraves and Harry Secombe, many other postwar stars developed or honed their comedy skills in the Forces, some in official entertainments units, others in less formal canteen shows. They formed the majority of the new comics as television became established as the principal source of popular entertainment.

Tommy Cooper

It was while serving in the army in the Middle East that Tommy Cooper first adopted the fez that became his trademark. It happened at a NAAFI concert in Cairo when Sgt Cooper mislaid the pith helmet that he intended to wear for his magic act and snatched a fez from an Egyptian waiter before going on.

Cooper's act was a series of conjuring tricks which went disastrously wrong. He would cover his confusion with a manic cackle until he was finally left surveying the chaos with eyes staring and mouth agape. He bungled the tricks deliberately, for he was actually a skilled magician respected by fellow members of the Magic Circle. Setting up three tables with more than a hundred of his props, every one in the right place, took an assistant more than an hour. At the end of his act it looked as if a bull had been set loose in a magic shop, but the disorder was carefully orchestrated.

He was a huge, lumbering man, 6 ft 4 in tall and more than 15 stone, with hands like earth-diggers and size 12 feet. He had a mobile face and spoke in a compulsive gabble as he kept up a running commentary on his act. 'Have a drink. I drink only for medicinal purposes; I'm sick of being sober. Look – glass, bottle, bottle, glass. Help yourself. A child of three can do this trick – and I wish he was here now. Ha, ha, ha . . . .' His catch phrase was, 'Just like that.'

He was born in Caerphilly, South Wales, in 1922 but brought up in Southampton where he took up magic at the age of nine when an aunt gave him some tricks. As a 17-year-old apprentice shipwright, he was invited by his employers to put on a show, but his nerves wrecked it. Every trick went wrong. Playing cards fell from his sleeves and sprayed from his hands, eggs smashed and his rabbit escaped and ran around the stage. The audience cried with laughter and his act was born.

He was seven years in the Horse Guards, claiming: 'I had a lazy horse. It didn't carry me. I had to carry him and I was the only trooper with saddle sore shoulders.' After leaving the army in 1947 he became a professional entertainer and spent two years touring variety theatres. In a season at London's Windmill Theatre he once did 52 shows in a week. His fortnightly TV series *It's Magic* began in 1952, following which he worked mainly in TV. After his series *Life with Cooper* in 1969 he was voted ITV Personality of the Year by the Variety Club.

He looked a riot. He could have gone on stage and just waved his hands and the audience would have roared, but he accompanied his magic with a string of throwaway jokes:

'Doctor, I've got a bad foot, what shall I do?' 'Limp.'

'Doctor, I've got no sense of direction.' 'Then get lost.'

'A woman told her doctor, "I've got a bad back." The doctor said, "It's old age." The woman said, "I want a second opinion." The doctor said, "OK, you're ugly as well."'

One of his routines involved trying to impersonate a policeman, a tramp and a bank

★ **Charlie Drake managed to bring chaos to every job he tackled in his series, *The Worker*, in which he played an unemployable. Here he gets involved with an automatic car wash ★**

★ Tommy Cooper's trademark was an Egyptian fez, which he first adopted for a wartime NAAFI concert in Cairo. The manic conjuror went on to wear one in innumerable television shows over more than 30 years ★

manager, and muddling their hats. Another had him playing two characters – such as a sailor and his wife – simultaneously by wearing halves of each costume.

He was a joker offstage as well, giving away ballpens inscribed, 'Stolen from Tommy Cooper'. He would press something into a cab driver's hand, saying, 'Have a drink on me.' When the recipient opened his hand later he would find a teabag. Ernie Wise remembers Cooper would take a foaming pint of beer, stick his chin in it so that he had a white beard of froth, and whine, 'You wouldn't hit an old man, would you?'

He died in 1984 aged 62, after collapsing on stage during a live TV show.

Norman Wisdom

Norman Wisdom joined the army at 15 as a band boy in the 10th Hussars and first learned the clarinet and then the piano, xylophone, saxophone, violin and trumpet. He was an underdog because of his small size; he was less than 5 ft tall and little more than 5 ½ stone at the time, but he acquired a reputation as a jester and joined an army concert party. Within months he was the chief comic. He taught himself falls, acrobatics, patter and singing, all

of which he was later to feature on television, along with shadow boxing which he practised on the way to becoming flyweight champion of the Hussars at 18.

He was born in North London in 1920 but his parents split up when he was nine and he lived with a guardian – when he was not running away. After leaving school at 14 he was a trainee waiter, but then walked from London to Cardiff to seek a job in a coalmine. Instead, he found his way to the docks and became a seasick cabin boy on a ship to Argentina.

When he left the army in 1946 after 11 years service he toured music halls in twice-nightly shows, living in a caravan. The ill-fitting, too-tight 'gump suit' that became his trademark was first seen at the Spa Theatre in Scarborough after conjuror David Nixon, who was on the same bill, asked him to help by going on stage as a member of the audience. The following day he bought a crumpled suit and battered cap, and he and Nixon were subsequently booked as a double act at the London Casino.

The upturned peak to the cap came later in an ITV show. The director told him to take the cap off because it was casting a shadow on his face. Wisdom protested that it was an import-

★ Norman Wisdom's trademark was his too-tight 'gump suit', first acquired to wear while acting as a conjuror's stooge in the Forties, and later in many series on television ★

ant part of his costume. The director said, 'Well, don't let's quarrel. Just turn the peak up.'

He made his first TV appearance in 1948 and was in his first Royal Variety Performance in 1952 which led to his own series a year later. In the same year he made the first of many film farces, *Trouble in Store,* in which he was seen causing chaos in a department store and singing *Don't Laugh at Me 'Cause I'm a Fool.* The song, which he wrote himself, became the theme of his act which leaned on pathos and falls, though he complained: 'People have always exaggerated the number of times I fall down. Some critics have implied that I play everything on my stomach.'

In 1961 a *Sunday Night at the London Palladium* show was virtually given over to him. He was on stage alone, apart from compere Bruce Forsyth, for most of the whole hour. There were no supporting acts, which was explained by a running joke about their non-arrival. Even the *Beat the Clock* game segment was shortened. Wisdom and Forsyth rehearsed 12 days for the show, which included a silent routine with Wisdom wallpapering and Forsyth as foreman, and climaxed with a chase through the audience and orchestra. Wisdom also mimed getting beaten up, played a variety of instruments and sang *Me and My Imagination.*

Wisdom hung up his gump suit for his 1970 series, *Norman,* to play a tax inspector who hated taking money from the public and wanted to become a musician, but returned to knockabout in later series including *A Little Bit of Wisdom.*

Benny Hill

Benny Hill was carried off to join the army by military police, who arrested him in Cardiff. It was not his fault; he was working in touring revues and his call-up papers had never reached him. In the army he was first a driver/mechanic but by 1941 had transferred to a *Stars in Battledress* company of entertainers.

Today he is the most famous comedian in the world, known through television in 80 countries. International fame came to him in 1979 when a number of his hour-long shows, made over 10 years, were re-edited into half-hours, omitting totally indigenous references, and sold to America. The Americans took to his nudge and wink humour; his programmes were screened twice nightly on some stations.

His success abroad is largely due to the visual

nature of his comedy. The podgy comic is seen as a dirty old man pursuing gorgeous girls – though never achieving any success with them. There are blue sketches and songs derived from old jokes, delivered with a cheeky grin. These offend many, and have been denounced as sexist and smutty – not only by women – but Hill regards them as being in the same tradition as saucy seaside postcards.

He writes his own material and this is one reason he makes only three new hour-long shows a year and never performs on stage. The others, he readily admits, are that he enjoys spending his time travelling and lounging in the sun. He likes to roam the Camargue and potter in old Roman towns like Nîmes and Arles. He speaks good French and can also converse in Spanish and German. He has no need to work for he has made more than 50 one-hour shows over 16 years, which have been packaged into more than 80 half-hour programmes.

He was born in Southampton in 1925, the son of a surgical appliance fitter (which sounds like the cue for a Hill gag) and grew up in a terraced house. His grandfather took him to see touring revues with such titles as *Cheeky Days, Don't Be Saucy* and *Naughty But Nice,* and he wanted to be the comic. At 14 he joined a semi-pro concert party and wore one of his father's collars back to front as a vicar. He was paid half a crown (12 ½ p).

He left school at 15 in the year war broke out and was a stockroom clerk at Woolworth's before he began a milk round with a horse and cart. At the same time he developed a Max Miller type of routine. Anxious to become established before his call-up, he headed for London with a cardboard suitcase in 1940 and slept on Streatham Common, first on grass, then in a partly built air raid shelter, until he found a job as assistant stage manager at East Ham Palace.

After the war, unable to get bookings, he wrote some sketches for TV, which was just beginning to make an impact. He took them to Ronnie Waldman, head of Light Entertainment at the BBC, and was offered some TV appearances which led to his own show, after which he abandoned the theatre for TV and has rarely been on a stage since.

He is unmarried and has few friends. He owns a flat in central London to which he carries home food to cook for himself, and rarely entertains. He has no interest in possessions other than his collection of videos of old comedies and does not

★ For a change, a picture of Benny Hill without scantily clad girls, though they were probably not far away, for the pursuit of girls is the mainstay of his comedy ★

own a car. No one appears to know him well.

Charlie Drake

Charlie Drake says he volunteered for the Royal Navy because it had a prettier uniform, but it declined to take him, and he joined the RAF instead, and spent most of his time doing shows. It was while in the RAF during the war that Drake met Jack Edwardes, then a RAF pilot, on an airfield in Northern Ireland. Edwardes was tall while Drake is a mere 5 ft 1 ½ in – 'I was raised on condensed milk,' he jokes – and their different sizes prompted an officer to say, 'You two ought to be a double act.'

They remembered the words when they met again by chance after the war at an audition where both had been unsuccessful. They went for a cup of tea and became *Mick and Montmorency,* stars of comedy programmes for children.

The roly-poly man with the greeting 'Hello my darlings' was born Charles Springall in London's Elephant and Castle district in 1925, one of seven children, of whom four survived. His father sold newspapers and collected street bets, his mother went out scrubbing, and Drake was singing at South London Palais to supplement the family income at the age of eight. At 10 he left school and took all kinds of jobs including polishing tombstones.

After the war he got a spot in *The Benny Hill Show* and received his first press notice. It praised Hill, and added: 'There was only one thing that was a stinker and that was Charlie Drake's sketch.' However, the BBC invited him to come up with more ideas, and *Mick and Montmorency* was one of the first. His comedy usually involved strenuous physical action. In *Drake's Progress* in 1958 he became entangled with apache dancers and knocked about by American gangsters. His stunts became wilder. His mind seethed with stunts – jumping, swinging, falling. 'I don't want giggles or chuckles,' he declared. 'What I need from an audience is the sound you hear when you're sitting by the sea at high tide and the waves are crashing on the beach. Whoomp! Whoomp! It's a belly laugh coming from deep down inside.'

He used to dream stunts, then talk them into a tape recorder by his bedside in a small flat in Leicester Square. He never rehearsed the stunts. 'If I did I'd be so scared I wouldn't be able to go through with them,' he claimed. 'I do them once and once only.' One stunt, when he crashed through a bookcase, was nearly fatal; he fractured his skull and was out of action for two years. He took up painting, and later had exhibitions of his contemporary oils.

His greatest television success was *The Worker* in which he played an unemployable, getting a new job every week from job centre manager, Mr Pugh (which Drake pronounced 'Poo'), played by Henry McGhee, and then making a mess of it. But Drake's career went into limbo when he became embroiled in a dispute with Equity, the actors' union, after he insisted on employing a

★ Charlie Drake in a comedy show (above) and in a drama (right). The acting role was in an *Armchair Theatre* play ★

talent contest winner in his 1974 Christmas pantomime in Bradford. She was not an Equity member and they fined him. When he refused to pay, as a matter of principle, he was banned from appearing in provincial theatres and was out of work for a year.

He moved into straight acting. 'I wasn't getting a kick out of comedy any more,' he said, 'and I feel that if you're not getting something from what you do you should stop it.' He says he likes the fact that in the classics no rewriting is required; the text is perfect. He won an acting award in *The Caretaker* and in 1981 played Shakespeare for the first time, as Touchstone in *As You Like It* on an open-air stage at Ludlow Festival. It was, he said, 'the most rewarding part I have ever done'.

Bob Monkhouse

Even after the war ended, conscription continued and would-be comics went on developing their talents in the Services. Bob Monkhouse, for example, was too young to serve in the war but was called up for national service after it, and made enterprising use of an RAF posting to an office in London as secretary to a Group Captain. After one radio date with Ralph Reader's *Gang Show* in 1947 he wrote to the BBC asking for an audition and was told to wait a year. 'The next letter I wrote was on office paper and purported to come from the Group Captain,' he recalls. 'I slipped it under a pile of other things for him to sign and off it went. The letter said that Cpl Monkhouse desperately needed an audition to boost his crumbling confidence. The BBC offered one at once.'

He passed, went on to appear regularly in radio hits such as *Variety Bandbox, Showtime* and *Workers' Playtime,* and was invited to write the script for *Calling All Forces.* 'At first I went on in civvies but I soon realised I got a bigger round of applause from the studio audience if I was wearing uniform, so I wore it.'

He has been called 'Mr Smarm,' and described as having a smile by Brylcreem. He is smooth, clever, fast-talking and quick with a quip. He is dapper and looks younger than his age. He is also a show business phenomenon.

He was born in 1928 in Beckenham, Kent, then very select and quiet. 'You weren't allowed to mix health salts after 7 at night,' jokes Monkhouse. 'You had to go three miles out of town to hiccup.' He recalls a happy childhood in which he never wanted for anything. His father was a chartered accountant, chairman of a custard company, and his mother was a painter. He was sent to Dulwich public school. When he first became a comic he concealed this comfortable background. 'A comedian was supposed to be of the people. If you said you had a car you lost them.'

As a boy he was shy. 'My shyness wasn't helped by my being a real fatty,' he says. 'At 11 I weighed 11 stone and you know how cruel schoolboys can be. The only way to win them over was to deliberately make them laugh at me. That way the sound of their laughter became a kind of success symbol.'

At 12, a wartime evacuee in the country, he began writing adventure stories in bed after blackout with a torch. 'One of the first thrillers I wrote was called *The Foul Death of Silas Grudge, Human Spider.* It didn't sell but many of my other works did.' He was an accomplished artist and sold his first strip cartoon to a children's comic when he was 11. By the time he was 15 he was a regular contributor to boys' magazines. Then he tried writing jokes for comedians, the first of which, about an old maid's drawers, he sold to Max Miller. He waited at a stage door in Lewisham for three hours in the rain to make the sale, and Miller paid him half a crown.

He began work as a film cartoon animator but then came his national service during which he began broadcasting for the BBC. In the RAF in London he started writing for radio stars Bonar Colleano, Harold Berens and Derek Roy. After his demob the BBC gave him a contract as a scriptwriter and he poured out gags and scripts and, in partnership with Denis Goodwin – another old boy of Dulwich College, though they had never met there – wrote for Arthur Askey, Ted Ray, Bob Hope, Jack Benny, Dean Martin and Jerry Lewis. Between them they wrote more than 2,000 radio scripts. The Monkhouse speciality was flip one-liners such as these:

'Diets are for people who are thick and tired of it.'

'Don't put off until tomorrow what you can do today. If you like it you can always do it again tomorrow.'

'If you see a person without a smile give him one of yours.'

'When a girl marries a man for his money she may spend the rest of her life looking for a little change.'

★ Bob Monkhouse leads a choir in extolling the joys of television in *The Bob Monkhouse Comedy Hour* on ITV in 1972. The multi-talented ex-corporal has been a cartoonist, a gag writer for other comics, a stand-up comedian, a star of situation comedy, and a presenter of game shows and talent shows. At one time he was on screen almost every night of the week ★

'There's nothing wrong with teenagers today that reasoning with them won't aggravate.'

Monkhouse wrote and starred in his first BBC TV series, *Fast and Loose,* in 1954 and two years later was on the screen almost every night of the week. He was in *My Pal Bob, The Bob Monkhouse Hour, Candid Camera* and *Startime* and in the game shows, *What's My Line?, Do You Trust Your Wife?* and *For Love or Money.* His ubiquity led a TV critic to refer to television as 'Monkhouse with knobs on'. He was also making films.

In the mid-Sixties a dip in his popularity coincided with the end of his writing partnership with Goodwin. One of his hobbies came to his aid. He has been acquiring vintage films since he was given his first projector by his father at 16, and claims to have the finest collection of old comedy films in the world. In 1965 in *Mad Movies* he presented a series of excerpts from them. Then he began a new stage in his career hosting game shows, including *The Golden Shot, Celebrity Squares, Family Fortunes* and *Bob's Full House,* and presenting *Bob Says . . . Opportunity Knocks.*

81

PALLADIUM NIGHTS

★

Sunday Night at the London Palladium began at 8 pm on September 25, 1955 with Gracie Fields and Guy Mitchell sharing top billing. The TV audience was estimated at 387,000, a figure that today would not even excite producers of off-peak programmes on Channel 4, but then ITV was just three days old and available only in the London area.

As the years passed more transmitters opened and in 1960 the average audience was 17 million, though in February of that year Max Bygraves drew 21 million and in December Harry Secombe a record 22 million. Sunday Night at the London Palladium was constantly in the Top Ten ratings. The programme that opened with the sound of Startime and ended with the artists riding the Palladium's great 'revolve' or turntable was more than the nation's favourite variety show; it was a 20th-century rite, determining the Sunday evening habits of almost half the nation's population. A Woking vicar recognised the fact when he brought Sunday evensong forward half an hour so that the congregation could get home in time to watch the programme. 'It's no use hiding the fact that Sunday Night at the London Palladium is more popular than going to church on a cold winter's night,' he said philosophically.

The compere's job was the top job in comedy. Tommy Trinder – catch phrase 'You lucky people' – was the first. One of his gags was: 'The army made a man out of Liberace – and he sued them.' Trinder has recalled: 'The next morning you couldn't see my desk for letters of protest from his fans.' Trinder's finest hour, however, was the night when a power failure postponed TV transmission of the show and he held the stage alone, cracking gags to keep the audience in their seats. The reported duration of his monologue – in which, he has said, he told every joke he could remember and

then invented new ones – has grown with the passage of the years, but contemporary accounts rated it between 75 and 90 minutes. When the show finally reached the screen his opening words to viewers were, 'Welcome to Monday morning at the Palladium.'

Trinder was followed as compere by Dickie Henderson, Bob Monkhouse, Hughie Green and – a slightly surprising choice – the portly actor and wit, Robert Morley. The job was later to create three major stars.

Bruce Forsyth

The first big new star created by the Palladium show was Bruce Forsyth, who came to it in 1958 from the bucket-and-spade circuit of summer shows at resorts including Babbacombe in Devon and Eastbourne in Sussex. A garage owner's son, the lantern-jawed Forsyth was born in Edmonton, London, in 1928, made his variety debut at 14 as Boy Bruce, the Mighty Atom, and was later a warm-up comic at the Windmill. He was versatile, exuberant and self-confident, tap dancing, playing piano, singing and joking, He duetted with the greatest and was never outclassed.

'I remember one show in which I danced with Sammy Davis,' he has told me. 'We never rehearsed but got together only at the Palladium. I think my dancing surprised him. Then I did a double act with Nat King Cole where we had two pianos on stage and played and sang, but those were live shows; they didn't videotape in those days and I haven't even got a sound tape as a memento.'

One of the compere's jobs was presenting the games interlude called Beat the Clock from which

★ Undoubtedly swinging! Norman Vaughan in his time as compere of Sunday Night at the London Palladium. He appeared in more than 100 programmes ★

82

everyone took away a prize. Contestants were usually pairs, a husband and wife or an engaged couple. They might be blindfolded and required to find each other and embrace within a time limit, guided only by kissing noises, or they might be required to don baggy trousers and wellingtons while keeping a balloon in the air. Common props were tennis balls, cups and saucers.

Viewers argued fiercely whether some games were possible to win. One in 1959 required a man to bounce a ball off a bass drum on to a snare drum and a cymbal to be caught by his partner. To prove to the audience that it was possible Forsyth attempted it and succeeded, but in 18 weeks no contestants managed it. The game was withdrawn and the prize money, which had reached £1,800, was divided between four charities. Three years later the game was brought back and won in the second week.

Forsyth, with his infectious grin, was in his element with *Beat the Clock*. 'Right, my love, don't be nervous,' he would say. 'All you have to do is arrange the words on the board into a well known phrase or saying. You have 30 seconds to beat the clock, starting from now .... You've done it! Well done, my love. Open the curtains. ... Marvellous! You have won to-night's star prize, a magnificent 18-inch television with press button controls.'

A woman contestant named Beattie argued in a good-humoured way with Forsyth while ignoring his instructions on how games should be played. Forsyth shouted in mock petulance: 'Listen Beattie, I'm in charge here.' The words 'I'm in charge' became a national catch phrase and appeared on lapel badges and foremen's helmets.

Forsyth came on with the force and subtlety of a battering ram and just as irresistibly. His confidence was awe-inspiring. He bullied and cajoled, mugged and strutted, his grin a yard wide. He insulted members of the audience and they loved it. He stayed for two years until his health cracked, when he was replaced by another unknown – the late Don Arrol, who had a fondness for complicated props, one of the most remarkable being a coat that unfolded into a boat complete with oars. While Forsyth could shout, 'I'm in charge,' and look it, Arrol appeared boyish and nervous and the hearts of viewing mothers went out to him.

Forsyth returned, restored in 1961, and by 1965 was starring in his own shows. They led to the BBC's *The Generation Game* in 1975 which involved games such as folding hats, creating action paintings and making cakes. It was in this series that he coined the catch phrases, 'Nice to see you, to see you ... nice' (which became his standard greeting) and, 'Didn't he do well?' (said admiringly after a contestant's performance). 'Good game ... good game,' was used to encourage audience enthusiasm, and 'Give us a twirl' was his invitation to Anthea Redfern, his hostess, who became his second wife, to display her dress of the week.

At his peak in 1976 and 1977, when he was TV Personality of the Year in the polls, his presence was sure to enliven the limpest show, his name alone guaranteed to pull a massive figure. He was a phenomenon, a wonder man of British television. Yet Forsyth wanted more. In 1977 he made a double LP record, *Both Sides of Bruce*. One disc consisted of an excerpt from his remarkable one-man show, recorded live at the Palladium that year before 2,500 people. 'They ran out of tape,' Forsyth said mendaciously to explain why it did not contain the whole virtuoso performance involving singing, dancing and audience manipulation, running to nearly three hours.

The other disc had Forsyth singing, and he delivered a song as confidently and professionally as he did everything else. The record was important to him for what he wanted was to reach an audience beyond Britain, where he was sure of his adoration, to become Bruce Forsyth, international superstar. 'I don't think I could ever live in America because my roots are here but I would like to go over there and steal a few dollars,' he told me. However, as he said realistically: 'Nobody gets to Las Vegas as an unknown. People only get invited when they are big recording stars, or in films, on American television or on Broadway.'

He had made films. In *Star!* in 1968 he danced with Julie Andrews but by this time he discounted films. 'I would have been ideal for musical films,' he said without false modesty, 'but the bottom has fallen right out of the market because they are so expensive to produce. Being a musical person there are all kinds of parts I could play, but they are just not making films like that any more, and I am certainly not taking my clothes off. You are better off not doing films than taking small roles in them.'

So he pinned his faith to records and television spectaculars with American stars whose names could sell them to American networks. On one ITV show, *The Entertainers* in 1977, he was partnered by Rita Moreno, tempestuous dancing star of *West Side Story*. 'Just the two of us and 16 dancers,' he recalls. 'We went out to dinner to see how we got on, because when you do that kind of show it becomes a sort of marriage. You have to give and take an awful lot but I am very adaptable, being Pisces and easily led. Well, we didn't throw any food at each other so we did the show, which was great.' They appeared together in the course of it as Antony and Cleopatra, Tarzan and Jane, Rudolph Valentino and Clara Bow.

He told me in 1977: 'I get bored very quickly doing the same thing, and I still have some ambitions left which is nice, because if you have been in the business as long as I have and you run out of ambition or things to do, then it is time to turn it in. I have realised so many ambitions in this country but if you can do something international it gives you a new slant to your work. More than anything else I'd like some international acclaim.'

But then his career suffered a setback. *Bruce Forsyth's Big Night* in 1979 was a disaster. It was a two-hour show designed to wrest Saturday night audiences back from the BBC, which dominated them with *The Generation Game* presented by Larry Grayson, followed by *Starsky and Hutch*. The juggernaut show involved a big star interview by Forsyth, a game show, a quiz, Charlie Drake in *The Worker*, Patricia Brake and Ian Lavender in *The Glums*, and much more. It was not Forsyth's fault that it bombed. He was better than the show, declared viewers; the marathon was a misconceived idea. From sixth in the ratings it dropped to 20th and sank from sight. At the same time Larry Grayson and *The Generation Game* continued in fourth place.

The Big Night ended and Forsyth got to America finally to make his Broadway debut with a show which included a games segment. Unaccountably, when presenting two bottles of champagne to contestants he cracked: 'The champagne's flat ... it was made in New York.' There were hisses from the audience.

The Butchers of Broadway – the critics – minced him. Then his second marriage broke up. In 1983 he married Puerto Rican Wilnelia Merced, a former Miss World, 30 years younger than himself.

He starred as a supermarket manager in *Slinger's Day*, a sitcom which he inherited after the death of Leonard Rossiter, who had starred in the original series titled *Tripper's Day*, but in recent years on TV he has concentrated on hosting game shows such as *Play Your Cards Right* and *You Bet!*

Norman Vaughan

Forsyth's replacement on the Palladium show in 1962 was another comparative unknown – Norman Vaughan. His two catch phrases 'Swinging' (accompanied by a thumbs-up sign) and 'Dodgy' (accompanied by a thumbs-down) were echoed all over the country in reaction to good or bad news.

Vaughan, born in 1927 in Liverpool, left school at 14, and made his stage debut the same year in revue with the Eton Boys Choir. They wore red jackets and jodhpurs and sang *D'ye Ken John Peel*. At 15 he formed his own trio, the Dancing Aces, and toured until his call-up for the army in 1945. As Sergeant Vaughan in Italy and the Middle East he performed in army shows with Harry Secombe and Spike Milligan.

In 1951 he toured the country in variety shows on the same bill as Secombe and went on to spend two years with a show in Australia. When he returned to England in 1955 he went into *Twinkle* in summer seasons at the seaside. As the Fifties turned into the Sixties he was touring as compere of a show starring Cliff Richard.

He was unknown but he was 34 years old and vastly experienced when he took over at the Palladium from Forsyth, but Forsyth was 'a hell of an act to follow', as he put it. On his debut in 1962 there were 20 million watching. 'I was paralysed with nerves,' he admitted, 'but overnight I was a personality. Taxi drivers would stick their thumbs up and say "Swinging" or "Dodgy".' He went on to star in more than 100 programmes over three years.

Later he gave viewers another catch phrase: 'Roses grow on you', during five years of commercials for chocolates, but his last TV series was as host of *The Golden Shot*, which he took over from Bob Monkhouse in 1972, though he co-devised the quiz show *Bullseye* in 1981, which Jim Bowen hosted. He has since acted in stage comedies including *Boeing-Boeing* and *A Bedful of Foreigners*, and has appeared in pantomimes and summer seasons.

Jimmy Tarbuck

The era of the Beatles and all things Liverpudlian produced Jimmy Tarbuck, who says his favourite place on earth is 'Anfield stadium, watching Liverpool FC', and his sporting heroes are 'anyone who has played for Liverpool'.

He first swaggered on to the Palladium stage in a Sunday night show in 1963. He was an unknown 23-year-old but was an instant hit. 'I was meant to go on for six minutes and carried on for nine, but I was just a boy and had no idea,' he recalls. Xavier Cugat and his band, who were topping the bill, had their act cut to make time for him. Two years later he took over as resident compere. 'Caviar butties all round,' he declared.

He was born in 1940, the son of a bookmaker and was at school with John Lennon and George Harrison. He left school at 15 and started work as a garage mechanic but was sacked from this and subsequent jobs for 'fooling around'. He became the compere of a touring rock show and then a Butlin's Redcoat, turning professional in 1963 and working in clubs in Liverpool and Manchester. His TV debut was that year in *Comedy Bandbox*.

During one *Sunday Night at the London Palladium* a temperamental Judy Garland sat in her dressing room deciding whether to go on while the band played *Over the Rainbow*, her introductory music, again and again. Tarbuck eventually coaxed her. On another occasion he forgot the name of Petula Clark and had to introduce her as 'someone who needs no introduction'.

Over the years he has had a succession of his own series on TV: *It's Tarbuck, Tarbuck's Back* and *Tarby and Friends* and returned to the Palladium as host of *Live From the London Palladium*. He has also presented the game shows *Winner Takes All* and *The Frame Game*. He is reputedly Britain's highest paid comic, with homes in England and Spain. The Queen has invited him to lunch at Buckingham Palace and Margaret Thatcher welcomed him to a function at 10 Downing Street.

Tarbuck has a theory that you can't start being really funny about life until you've lived a bit of it. 'I did very well as a young lad but I don't think I really came into my own until I turned 40. What improves with your age is your timing.'

In 1988 I asked him to name his Top Ten comics. The list was Eric Morecambe, Max Miller, Tommy Cooper, Laurel and Hardy, The Two Ronnies, Victoria Wood, Billy Connolly, Bob Hope, Russ Abbot and Woody Allen, with special mentions for Phil Silvers and Richard Digance. It was noticeable that he did not include any new wave or alternative comics. He is reputed to find them about as funny as Aids, though he told me: 'That's not true. That's the Press making statements and altering statements that I've made. I think Rik Mayall is a very talented person and very funny, but I think some of the charge-and-shout brigade aren't, and I don't want to hear rude words 10 times in a night and see them pick their noses.' The dislike is returned. To TV's new wave comedians 'Tarbuck and his golfing pals' represent all they detest in comedy.

Des O'Connor

Although he was not actually discovered by the Palladium show, Des O'Connor was a frequent stand-in for Don Arroll, Norman Vaughan and Bruce Forsyth. The man with the boyish grin and dimples makes entertaining look easy. He once said he did not do anything sensational, but did not offend or embarrass, and was occasionally quite funny.

He was born in Stepney in London in 1932. His father was a drayman at a local brewery and later a milkman. As a child O'Connor was undersized. He suffered from rickets and wore irons on one leg until he was six or seven. He also developed diphtheria and scarlet fever and was run over twice. The second time he was dragged along beneath a car and was nearly a year in hospital.

His home in the East End was destroyed in the 1940 blitz, after which he was evacuated and went to live in Northampton, where he discovered fields and sport and began to grow. At 14 he began work as complaints clerk in a shoe factory in Northampton. At 18 he joined the RAF for two years national service, went to a holiday camp on leave, entered all the competitions and won most. The manager offered O'Connor a job on his demob in 1952 and he spent two years as a Redcoat at Filey. His main work was as a sports organiser rather than an entertainer. Once he took 60 pensioners on a beach ramble and got them trapped by the incoming tide, and when he buried treasure in sand for children to find he forgot where he buried it.

According to his own account, he bribed the camp comic to let him take the stage but was fired for reciting a rude limerick. After his reinstatement he was in charge of a sing-song when he saw a man in the aisle and told him he could not stand there because it was against fire regulations. 'But I'm Billy Butlin,' said the man, to which O'Connor replied: 'I'm the Queen of Sheba. Out!' Next day Butlin called him into his office and complimented him for upholding regulations.

O'Connor made his professional debut at the Palace Theatre, Newcastle, in 1953 before an audience of six usherettes and 14 customers. He says he was originally a frantic comic but suffering from a bout of food poisoning when appearing in Guernsey, he did not even dare

★ 'Deaf' O'Connor, (as he was called by Eric Morecambe) ★

laugh, performed his whole act quietly and found it went better. In 1963 after compering *Sunday Night at the London Palladium* he was given his own TV series, *Des O'Connor Tonight* and *Des O'Connor Live* in which he combined comedy, singing and chat show elements. In one programme Freddie Starr hit him on the head with the microphone. O'Connor took it back and hit Starr harder.

He has made a number of hit records including *Careless Hands* (his first million seller), *I Pretend* (his second) and *One, Two, Three O'Leary*, and has won nine gold discs and sold 11 million albums worldwide – despite jibes about his singing. 'Jack Benny had mean jokes and Dean Martin drunk jokes. With me it's Des-is-an-awful-singer jokes,' he says. 'I can't get in a cab without the driver grinning and saying "I'll take you if you promise not to sing."'

Eric Morecambe started the jokes in the Sixties. Morecambe called him 'Deaf' O'Connor, and alleged 'Des' was short for 'Desperate'. Other comics joined in the abuse. O'Connor claimed to have counted 13 insults in eight different shows one Christmas. In fact, O'Connor enjoyed them; he had provided many of the jibes delivered by Morecambe, who was a friend, though this was not apparent to viewers. When Morecambe was in hospital with heart trouble O'Connor made an emotional speech at the end of a show wishing him well. When Morecambe returned to work he said: 'I hear that Des O'Connor had both houses pray for me at the Festival Theatre. It was very touching. Those 16 or 17 people made all the difference.'

TV Times readers voted O'Connor their favourite male TV personality from 1969 to 1973.

Sunday Night at the London Palladium ran for 12 years – with breaks during summer, ending with an Anglo-American series hosted by stars including Lorne Greene and Roger Moore. The final show had Bob Monkhouse in the compere's job and the bill-toppers were three ex-comperes that the Palladium had made into stars – Forsyth, Vaughan and Tarbuck. The series was revived in 1973 with Jim Dale and later Ted Rogers as hosts but the old magic had gone, and it was not recaptured by the *Live from the Palladium* series fronted by Tarbuck in the Eighties.

★

THE ELECTRONIC AGE

★

The first television comedy show born of the electronic age, rather than being merely an updated version of music hall, was *Laugh-In*, which began in 1968 and was the fastest, liveliest and most original comedy show of its day. A tightly edited mix of short skits and one-liners, it flashed backwards and forwards, using black-outs and quick cuts, and influenced light entertainment all round the world.

Sammy Davis Jr appeared on the show several times but every time be began to sing he was dropped through a trap door. John Wayne walked on to utter the one line, 'Well, I don't think that is funny.' The production team approached every star who visited the Burbank studios for whatever reason; if they could be induced to spend an hour or two delivering some lines, the material could be chopped and distributed through a number of programmes. The pay was only nominal, but when the series became popular, international stars found brief guest appearances in it irresistible. Zsa Zsa Gabor was seen in 105 spots, Greer Garson in 70, Harry Belafonte in more than 50.

No show ever produced more catch phrases than *Laugh-In*. 'Is this the party to whom I am speaking?' asked Lily Tomlin every week as Ernestine, a snobbish, nasal switchboard operator. 'I forgot the question,' pouted Goldie Hawn as the archetypal dumb blonde. 'Verrry interesting . . . but stupid!' said Arte Johnson as a steel-helmeted German soldier behind a potted plant. Others included 'I'll drink to that' and 'You bet your sweet bippy!' said by Dick Martin, 'Hi, sports fans,' said by Alan Sues as a TV sports presenter, and 'Here come de judge,' said by 'Pigmeat' Markham. Most famous of the catch phrases though was 'Sock it to me!', spoken by British actress Judy Carne. Whenever she used it she would be hit by a bucket of water, or get a custard pie in the face.

Guest stars were sometimes induced to say

the line, though they were rarely subjected to similar indignities. Richard Nixon, running for the American Presidency in 1968, said 'Sock it to *me?*' In fact, he said it six times during recording, because he could not get the inflection right. For political balance, the same opportunity was offered to his Democratic rival, Hubert Humphrey, who declined.

Every show opened with announcer Gary Owens, hand cupped to ear, declaring: 'This is beautiful downtown Burbank.' Regular features included a cocktail party scene, the Flying Fickle Finger of Fate award (a prize in a mock talent contest), and a joke wall in which the cast opened and shut windows to call one-liners. *Laugh-In* had no political platform. It joked about serious issues but was not trying to change the world, nor was it cruel, though it was sometimes outrageous by the standards of its time. One item in its regular feature, News of the Future, read:

> Dateline: the Vatican 1988. With marriage in the Church now an accepted practice, the Archbishop and his lovely bride, the former Sister Mary Catherine, both announced that this time it's for keeps – if only for the sake of the children.

Rowan and Martin

Laugh-In made millionaires of its two hosts, Dick Martin, playing the idiot, and Dan Rowan, his sun-tanned, moustached straight man. Rowan, born in Beggs, Oklahoma, in 1922, and Martin, born in Detroit, Michigan, in 1923, had been partners since 1952 and had known lean days. For 15 years they had worked nightclubs and served as toastmasters at banquets. When Dean Martin and Jerry Lewis split up in the mid-Fifties Rowan and Martin were tipped to succeed them in film comedies but it never happened. However, they impressed as a summer replacement for Dean

★ Dan Rowan was the straight man, Dick Martin played the fool. Together they hosted *Laugh-In*, the most innovative comedy show of the Sixties ★

Martin's TV show in 1967, and the outcome was *Laugh-In*, which won four Emmy awards in its first year.

There were 140 *Laugh-Ins* between 1968 and 1973, after which Rowan and Martin went their own ways but remained on good terms. Martin became a TV director, while Rowan retired and settled in luxury on an island off the west coast of Florida. He spent six months of every year in the USA and the rest exploring European canals in his own barge, *Encore*, until he died of cancer in 1987.

Bernard Manning

Laugh-In inspired other series around the world. In ITV's *The Comedians*, created by John Hamp in 1971 and revived briefly in 1985, innumerable comics recorded their acts, which were then sliced and spliced and edited for pace. The series made stars of many little-known comedians, the most notorious of whom is Bernard Manning.

He has been called Britain's lewdest, crudest comic. He tells blue jokes and says that in *The Comedians*, 'I had to use cue cards because if a clean gag is not in front of me a dirty one comes out.' He tells jokes about the Irish. 'This Irishman went in to buy a pair of tortoiseshell shoes; he put them on and it took him four hours to walk out of the shop.' He tells jokes about Pakistanis. 'I've got a Paki neighbour; he says he's a better man than I am because he *doesn't* have a Pakistani neighbour.' On a *Parkinson* show Esther Rantzen criticised his jokes. Manning says: 'I suddenly went all serious and started to say something like there was nothing I would like better than to see all the world – the Irish, the Jews and so on come together, united, and she was lapping it up. Then, when I said, "... to attack the Pakis", her face fell.' He says he hates 'Holier-than-thou folk'. 'They bring out the devil in me.'

Manning insults members of the audience. He will tell a thin woman: 'I'll bet the dog kept burying you in the garden.' He will tell a large one: 'I used to be fat like you.' He will pick on an untidy man: 'You're a scruffy looking devil. Look at that shirt; I wouldn't let our dog lie down in that shirt.' For *Under Manning*, a game show he presented in 1981, Southern Television advertised for eccentrics who did not mind being insulted. They were. When one contestant said she was 75, Manning replied:

'You look every day of it. I'd have said you were about 83 myself.' Some contestants gave as good as they got. When Manning asked a 12-year-old boy (who played a trumpet with his nose) 'What do you want to be when you grow up?' the boy answered, 'A comedian. What do you want to be?'

Manning says: 'People love insult humour. The secret is they know I'm only kidding.' He heaps insults on his rivals: 'Charlie Williams is to comedy what Larry Grayson is to Rugby League. Bruce Forsyth should buy a taxi and earn a decent living. Jimmy Tarbuck doesn't tell gags, he just refreshes your memory. Ronnie Corbett? I wouldn't pay him in washers. Terry Wogan has all the warmth and charm of an unflushed toilet. Des O'Connor is so mean he pulled out his fags and a cigarette card of Stanley Matthews fell out.'

The comics reply in kind:

Lennie Bennett: 'I always love Bernard's act. It saves me having to take a sleeping pill.'

Frank Carson: 'I've always enjoyed his show; his joke is very good.'

Freddie Starr: 'Bernard has talent. God gave him a big mouth.'

Mike Reid: 'They tell a joke in the business: If Bernard Manning and a hippo fell off Blackpool tower who would hit the ground first? Who cares?'

Charlie Williams: 'If slagging people off is a gimmick, then it's a poor gimmick.'

Manning is giant-sized. Fuelled by mountains of chips, his weight has sometimes hovered on the 20-stone mark. 'My pallbearers will know they've carried a coffin,' he has declared. 'With my weight they'll think I died of lead poisoning.' Bob Monkhouse alleged: 'If he was in the condemned cell he'd ask for two last meals.' Colin Crompton who starred with Manning in *The Wheeltappers' and Shunters' Social Club* on ITV in 1974, joked: 'Manning gave his old clothes to Oxfam but they're still looking for a 24-stone starving African.'

He is pugnacious, looking on every encounter with an audience as a battle. 'I never leave the stage until they submit,' he says. When he was mugged of £7,000 outside his Manchester club he struck out with the money bag despite a gun pointing at his head and only went down when a second robber hit him with a pickaxe handle. Offstage he is normally friendly and well-mannered, and tells stories against himself such as one about a man who telephoned him and said: 'Arthur Askey, Eric Morecambe and Tommy Cooper are all dead; how are you? I've got you with them in a Yankee bet.'

Manchester-born Manning left school at 14 and his first job was putting cigarettes on a conveyor belt in a factory. Then he went into the fruit and vegetable trade with his green-grocer father, getting up at 4 am and taking a horse and cart to load cauliflowers and beans at market. At night he won talent contests as a ballad singer. At 17 friends entered him for a singing contest at a pub and he won a big doll which he gave his mother. During his national service he sang with the dance band of the Manchester Regiment and later was vocalist with the Oscar Rabin band in London.

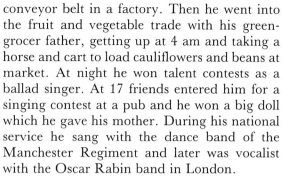

★ The man who has been called Britain's lewdest, crudest comic, Bernard Manning, one of the original stars of *The Comedians*. Insults are his speciality ★

He opened his first club with his father in 1959 in a former temperance billiard hall, providing a cheap, boozy night out with laughs. Manning presided like a genial Redcoat, with his sisters behind the bar, his mother on the till, his father in the cellar. Later he opened another, bigger one near by. Clubs are where he is in his element. He never takes a holiday and travels thousands of miles from club to club in his Rolls-Royce or Lincoln Continental, both of which have personalised number-plates. Television, he says, does not pay well, gags have to be scripted, rehearsals remove sponta-neity and there is a danger of over-exposure.

Ken Goodwin

By contrast, Ken Goodwin, another of the original *Comedians*, sets out to be a family comic. He specialises in schoolboy jokes taken from children's comics, their punchlines delivered almost apologetically:

★ 'I'm just Simple Simon,' says Ken Goodwin ★

'What happened to the cat who wore gloves? She had mittens.'

'I got on a bus in Manchester the other day and I said to the conductor, "Do you stop at the Imperial?" He said, "What – on my money?"'

'I took the dog for a walk the other day. A neighbour said, "Why's your dog wearing brown boots?" I said, "Because his black ones are at the menders."'

'I was driving along the other night when I was stopped by a policeman. "Would you mind blowing into this bag," he said. I replied, "What for?" "Well," he said, "me chips are too hot."'

'There were these two pillar boxes. One said to the other, "Let's get married." The other said, "Don't be daft, I'm a male box."'

It's cheek, he says. 'I don't know how I've got the nerve to tell terrible jokes like I do but it works. It's all in the character, the way I tell the jokes. I'm just Simple Simon. I come over all nervous and shy and most of the audience is laughing at me before I've said a word.'

He was born in 1933 in Manchester. His father was a stoker and he was outfitted with clothes from a local church. Idolising George Formby, he taught himself to play the ukulele and entertained in local clubs playing the uke and telling jokes while working successively as a coalman, travelling salesman, millworker and market gardener. His instrument playing ended when he hurt one of his hands putting up goalposts in a Manchester park; the crossbar slipped and crushed it badly. 'At the time I was heartbroken, but it turns out the accident did me a good turn,' he says.

His wife, Pat, encouraged him to enter a talent contest at Leek, Staffs, as a comic; he won £100 and turned professional. Pat gave him his catch phrase, 'Settle down', and his two daughters gave him jokes heard at school. After winning *Opportunity Knocks!* he was invited to join *The Comedians*, and was established, but his wife became ill in 1974 and he was forced to abandon his career to care for her and their daughters. After she died in 1977 he went back to work and has since remarried.

Frank Carson

'It's the way I tell 'em,' says Frank Carson, and he tells 'em with the unstoppability of a steamroller. He claims, 'I can out-talk anyone anywhere. I never dry up.' His eyes glint behind thick horn-rimmed glasses on his chubby face. The first comic seen in *The Comedians*, he jokes in the traditional way about 'the wife', mother-in-law and boarding house landladies.

'My wife talks through her nose,' he says. 'She goes on so much her mouth is worn out. And ungrateful! Do you know I gave her a chair for Christmas and she won't plug it in. A friend of mine said his wife was an angel. I said, "You're lucky, mine's still alive." The wife has been on to me for years to go to a sauna, so I said, "OK, let's go." We got to this place, stripped off . . . and when the steam cleared we found we were in a fish and chip shop.'

'That's a cracker,' he says admiringly when a joke goes well.

He was born in Belfast in 1926. His father was a dustbin man with the local council, a non-stop worker but unable to get a well-paid job and Carson never had a suit until he was 15. His first job was as an apprentice electrician but on his first day he put a pick through an electric cable and blacked out the north side of Belfast. He then worked as a plasterer by day and entertained in the evenings, standing outside the hall or club where he was to appear and handing out leaflets or selling tickets.

Crossing to England, he played summer seasons at holiday camps and then won *Opportunity Knocks!* which led to *The Comedians*. While he no longer has to hustle tickets to his shows, he still woos audiences attentively and will go into the bar of a theatre where he is performing, joke, buy drinks, sign autographs and kiss women. Being unrecognised makes him unhappy.

Charlie Williams

Charlie Williams, another of the first *Comedians*, is as Yorkshire as the pudding. He is also black. 'I'm coloured, with a broad Yorks accent,' he points out unnecessarily. 'You know, I really give the accent summat when I'm on stage. People say to me: "As soon as you started talkin' I fell off me chair." This is it, you see, I've got an unfair advantage.'

He was born near Barnsley. His father had come from Barbados to fight in World War One and stayed on as a miner. Williams himself started down a pit, repairing machinery. His escape was through football. He played wing-

★ Charlie Williams – as Yorkshire as the pudding, and black. 'An unfair advantage,' he says ★

★ The first comic seen in *The Comedians*, Belfast's Frank Carson, here dressed to promote ITV's charity show, *Telethon '88* ★

half, later centre-half, and won a reputation as a close marker. 'I weren't a good player but I were good enough to stop them that were,' he says. He became a semi-pro for Doncaster Rovers in 1949 when he was 19 and was then a full-time professional with them from 1953 to 1960, when the maximum wage was £20 a week.

'To be paid to keep fit weren't bad way to make a living,' he says. 'I liked training even in t'close season, and they were good crowds then, none of this shoutin' and bawlin' and cussin' and swearin'. If I were opposition I always knew if I was playing well. There was "Get back to Africa", and all that lot. When it was all over it were: "Well played, old love."'

In 1959 he was injured, with torn ligaments, and the following season he was transfer-listed at £3,500 and moved to Skegness for £15 a week. He had begun entertaining at supporters' social nights in Doncaster, singing Nat King Cole, Billy Eckstein, Billy Daniels and Sammy Davis numbers. In Skegness he began to add gags, having found that comics could earn more than singers. It came easily to him. 'As a kid I could always tell a yarn better than anybody else. It were a natural flair. I've always been a naturally happy person, always laughin' and likin' things lively.'

He continued to play soccer as a semi-pro and to work clubs as a sideline until 1970 when he turned professional comedian, with the catch phrases 'Now, me old flower', and 'Me old fruit'. In *The Comedians* he drew on childhood memories: 'Livin' in terraced row, toilets round back ... your mother used t'do washin' in copper on Monday, and on Tuesday you got same copper full of stew wi' dumplings and spare ribs.'

He also jokes about football, sex and colour. 'During the power cuts I had no trouble because all I had to do was roll my eyes,' he says, and, 'It was so sunny today I thought I'd been deported.' In a club he will call attention to people eating scampi: 'Look at this ... and they call us cannibals. Anyway I'm glad you're settling down in this country now.' He has been criticised for such jokes but he replies: 'Some of my ethnic jokes are against coloured people, some on whites, and that to my mind is healthy.' He was withering when asked his views about an attempt some years ago to outlaw the Golly label on pots of jam. 'Don't be so daft,' he said. 'I thought it was a good photograph.'

Tom O'Connor

Two comics who appeared in *The Comedians* had slightly surprising backgrounds. Tom O'Connor and Jim Bowen were teachers; both went on to front game shows. The prematurely grey O'Connor – he began to go grey at 15 – was a maths and music teacher in Bootle, on Merseyside, where he was born in 1939, and cherishes a pocket watch presented to him by the boys when he left. He began joking to keep the boys in his class in order and then started taking occasional paid engagements as a hobby. A £40 prize for winning a talent contest in a pub paid for his first guitar and for five years he played working men's clubs in Lancs while still teaching E stream maths.

One week he taught for five days and played three clubs each night. On the Saturday he appeared at two children's parties and four nightclubs. Then he slept for three days and missed two days at school. Unlike others on the club circuit, he told no dirty jokes, partly because of his Catholic upbringing, partly from a wish to be different. He invented characters including Superburk, who was going to save the country, and cloth-capped Arfur Woodie, never without a Woodbine in his mouth, and Happy Harry Wainwright Jr, winner of the Golden Clod award as worst entertainer of the year.

But the club circuit was hard. Once he travelled through snow to a club in Wales to find one man in the audience, but was required to go on. Playing a tough club in Manchester, filled with drunks, prostitutes and Norwegian sailors, and scared, he was advised by an old-time comic to write the punchlines of his gags on the side of fingers with a ballpen, so he could look at his cues while holding the mike. He tried it, but sweated so much from nerves the writing was obliterated.

After winning *Opportunity Knocks!* and appearing in *The Comedians* he achieved his own series, hosting *Wednesday at Eight* and *London Night Out*, which led to *The Tom O'Connor Show* and *Tom O'Connor at the Casino*, and he put schoolteaching behind him. Since then he has

★ Once he taught maths in Bootle; then Tom O'Connor became King of the Game Shows ★

become known as 'the king of game shows', presenting at least seven different ones, *The Zodiac Game, Name That Tune, Gambit, Password, I've Got a Secret, A Question of Entertainment,* and *Cross Wits,* which was five days weekly in 1988. Like other game show hosts, he enjoys the fact that two shows, and sometimes three, are recorded in a day. He once did six *Name That Tune*s. 'Brain damaging it was,' he says.

He claims Liverpool is the place to hear funny stories. He recalls taking a cab from Lime Street and asking the driver, 'Hard times in the city, then?' The cabbie answered: 'That's right Tom. I mean, it must be at least a fortnight since anyone was sick in the back of this cab.' Dockers telephone him with stories which he logs in his computer, stories like one about a Jewish tailoress who had been working at her machine all day. Walking home she came across a flasher, who opened his raincoat. She said, 'Call that a lining?'

Jim Bowen

Jim Bowen was deputy headmaster of a Lancashire primary school. Born in Heswall,

Cheshire in 1937, he was adopted by the foreman of a brickworks and his wife, a weaver, and grew up in a terraced house with no inside lavatory or bath. At Accrington Grammar School he sat nine O-levels and failed them all, but after doing odd jobs for a year he went back to school and passed them. He spent his national service as an army corporal and then went to teachers' training college and subsequently taught maths and physical education.

His first stage appearance was at a pub in Blackburn where the comic was awful. 'I bet a pal I could get more laughs than the other

★ **Jim Bowen away from TV in a hobby role as pub landlord – though not far away, for darts is the traditional pub game and on TV he hosts** *Bullseye* ★

feller,' he says. 'I failed miserably.' (Bowen is refreshingly honest about his performances.) But he became a part-time club entertainer and then went into *The Comedians*.

In 1981 he became presenter of *Bullseye*, ITV's darts-and-quiz game – and made an inauspicious debut. 'I made the contestants jumpy the moment I shook hands,' he says. 'I told jokes while they were trying to win, and stopped them after each throw to ruin their rhythm. Phyllis, my wife, put on a black armband and wept quietly. The kids went to fetch an oxygen bottle. The dog left home and our black cat turned grey.' But he improved, the show climbed the ratings charts, and he was able to create a home of character by converting a former railway station in Cumbria, and to buy matching his-and-hers Mercedes for himself and his wife.

NEW TALENT

★

The search for new talent for television goes on endlessly – in clubs and pubs and today in university revues – but the biggest showcase for new talent is television itself. Television's longest-running new-talent show was Hughie Green's *Opportunity Knocks!* (known in the business as *Opp Knox!*) which he presented from 1956 to 1977. Contestants were scored by the 'clapometer' activated by audience applause. When I talked to Hughie Green in 1976 at rehearsals for the 400th show he had then introduced some 2,000 acts and auditioned 120,000 more. 'The reason the show has lasted so long,' he said, 'is because the company insists, and so do I, that we give all the artists the best possible backing and presentation. We treat everyone in *Opp Knox!* like a star.'

A rival programme was *New Faces* which ran from 1973 to 1978, hosted by Derek Hobson, with a panel of show business judges, whose comments on acts were sometimes harsh. *New Faces* was brought back in 1986 with Marti Caine, who had been a winner in 1975, as presenter, after which the BBC revived *Opportunity Knocks!* with Bob Monkhouse as *Bob Says ... Opportunity Knocks*. These are some of the stars discovered in the programmes.

Les Dawson

Les Dawson rose to fame with jokes insulting his wife and mother-in-law. 'I'm not saying she's ugly but every time she puts make-up on the lipstick backs into the tube. . . . My mother-in-law hates me. She says I'm effeminate, and next to her, I am. . . . She never stops talking; her mouth's open so often we lag her tonsils in winter.'

His humour is based on woe and failure. 'I wouldn't say we were poor but we thought knives and forks were jewellery. . . . Life hasn't been easy; when I was a boy my family were so poor that Dad used to mug tramps. . . . We were

thrown out on the street so often we had loose covers made to match the pavement. . . . I wouldn't say it was a rough area but the kid next door shot his parents so he could go to the orphans' picnic. . . . Me dad's idea of a night out at a Chinese restaurant was begging for crusts outside a laundry.'

More recently he has joked: 'I got on a speak-your-weight machine and it said, "You are 14 stone 8, you have a sunny disposition and you're a big hit on *Blankety Blank*. . . ." It got my weight wrong too.'

He was born in Manchester in 1934. He came out of the army after national service with a first short story published in *Argosy*, and went to Paris to write. 'Dusk bled sepia-tinged over the stagnant Seine,' he mocks. He realised he needed other sources of income (though he has since written successful novels) and became a pianist in a Paris brothel. He was, he says, so naive it was weeks before he discovered it was anything more than a cabaret club.

He was equally unsuccessful at selling vacuum cleaners and washing machines in a slum area of Manchester and began to entertain in clubs. 'A comic was more like a human sacrifice,' he says. 'It was a matter of pride on the part of the audience to turn a normal human being into a quivering wreck in as short a time as possible.' He once suffered the ultimate indignity when the entire audience walked out half-way through his act. 'Now't to do with you,' explained the club chairman. 'The pies have come.' In another club he was just about to go on when men in black armbands mounted the stage. One said into the microphone: 'As you know, Harry, our chairman, passed on last

★ Lenny Henry, who had a meteoric rise to stardom after winning *New Faces* as a 16-year-old impressionist. He has matured into a thoughtful comic ★

★ Les Dawson raises laughs with a woebegone expression and humour based on gloom and failure ★

night. Could we all now stand and observe two minutes' silence?' Then he announced, 'Now for our comic.' Dawson says, 'I died too.'

His was then a bright and breezy act, but on his last night after a week in a Hull club he had a few drinks, slumped against the piano and moaned about the wretchedness of life as a comic. 'I don't have to do this for a living,' he told the audience. 'I just do it for luxuries like bread and shoes,' and they roared. He had a new act, but it earned him no more than a living in pubs and clubs. In 1967 he saw *Opp Knox!* as a last chance. He won and his ITV series, *Sez Lez*, followed. His first Royal Variety Performance in 1971 is still his favourite memory. In 1984 he took over *Blankety Blank* from Terry Wogan.

Dawson stands 5 ft 6½ in tall and weighs around 15½ stone. The face, which so often suggests depression and fatigue, is mobile and he can contort it into grotesque shapes. 'I can't help my face,' he says. 'I just have this hang-dog look. Years ago I realised I'd never be a womaniser with a face like this so I make people laugh instead.'

He writes most of his own material, which contains uniquely florid passages, for example: 'We had a lovely wedding. The rays of the sun filtered through the stained-glass windows of the medieval chapel, highlighting the mellow architecture of the Saxon altar and glinting off her father's loaded shotgun. . . .' In real life his publicly much-maligned wife, the woman he called privately 'my darling Meg, my rock, my tower of strength', died of cancer in 1986 after 25 years of marriage. At the funeral the vicar read words written by Dawson: 'She walks in the warmth of eternal sunshine and sleeps where no shadows fall.'

Russ Abbot

Russ Abbot was an *Opportunity Knocks!* winner when he was a member of the Black Abbots group, before he became a star under his own name. He still likes to work in a group, says he could not do a stand-up routine and has never played himself. He finds inspiration in costumes and props. 'I'm just myself until I put on a wig, then madness takes over,' he says.

One of his first comedy characters was a Boy Scout. He had found flapping khaki shorts in an Oxfam shop and added a khaki shirt, green socks and a few badges. He shouted 'Dib, dib, dib,' and audiences shouted back, 'Dob, dob, dob.' He has since opened Scout fêtes in that outfit, but is better known today as Jimmy, an orange-haired, tartan-clad, Glaswegian head-butter, with a sporran comprising a saucepan and a plastic fried egg and sausage. Other Abbot characters include yodelling Fritz Crackers, Boggles, an intrepid airman, Cooperman, a skinny Tommy Cooper in Superman garb, Basildon Bond (a spy in a wet suit), mad, straitjacketed psychiatrist Hans von Meatball, and bungling sleuth Barratt Holmes and his friend Dr Wimpey.

Abbot was born in Chester, his real name Russell Roberts, and he was originally a drummer. As a small boy he lined up dinner plates and beat them with a spoon. His father, an area manager of an oil company, bought him his first drum kit when he was 12 to encourage him to work for his O-levels, but he formed a group and failed the exams. After leaving school he began to perform as a drummer in bands at the Royalty Theatre, Chester, where the manager asked for some comedy. It was an old theatre, and had a stock of props and costumes such as Roman togas. Abbot would pick out costumes and devise a sketch on Thursday and stage it on Sunday.

For 15 years he played drums and clowned with the Black Abbots in summer seasons and pantomimes, leaving them in 1980 for *Russ Abbot's Madhouse* on ITV. *TV Times* readers voted him 'the funniest man on television' from 1982 to 1984, after which he was lured to the BBC for *The Russ Abbot Show* on a promise of more lavish production. At the same time he moved home from Chester to London.

He uses a team of writers, though his jokes are unremarkable. A typical one: 'Two lunatics go to sleep in a field and cover themselves up with their bikes for warmth. Next morning one says, "I was freezing." The other replies, "No wonder; some of your spokes are missing."'' He still finds his inspiration in props, though sometimes they cause problems. Doing a Mick Jagger impersonation in a stage show, wearing

a flabby-lipped rubber mask, he breathed in heavily and sucked his false teeth down his throat. He fell to the floor, gurgling, while the audience, unaware that he was choking, rocked with laughter. A resourceful guitarist stuck his fingers down Abbot's throat – 'nearly losing his digital watch,' says the comic, and retrieved the dentures though not before Abbot had passed out.

His potential seems yet unfulfilled. In 1984 he made his West End debut in *Little Me*, playing nine different characters, and in 1987 starred in Willy Russell's play, *One for the Road*, as a 40-year-old seeking an escape from the boredom of suburban life. He tells the story against himself of how one night he heard Paul Newman, Joanne Woodward and Steven Spielberg were seen in the theatre foyer. 'Then Newman said, "I think we're in the wrong theatre," and they trooped out and went next door to see Sir John Gielgud.'

Tall and laid back, he has the ability to switch off away from theatre or studio, and is a solitary man away from his family.

Lenny Henry

Lenny Henry began his career by winning *New Faces* in 1975 when he was a 16-year-old pupil at a technical college in his native Dudley. 'You may have seen some of these impressions before, but not in colour,' he announced before imitating Michael Crawford as Frank Spencer. 'I was bending over a pram going, "Ooooh, Betty",' he recalls, 'and when I looked up you could hear the audience gasping, "Ooh, he's *black*."'

He was a sensation and within days left the college, giving up his engineering apprenticeship. Every working men's club wanted to book the 16-year-old. 'What they didn't know was I'd only six jokes and no act. I soon realised being young and black wasn't enough. The novelty wore off.'

He spent five years with the Black and White Minstrels – the only genuine black face on stage – and appeared in two series of ITV's *The Fosters*, the sitcom about a black family in London, then scored a big hit in *Tiswas*, moving on to its adult version, *OTT*, and joining Tracey Ullman and David Copperfield in *Three of a Kind*. He has had his own BBC series since 1984.

He still has a natural talent for imperson-

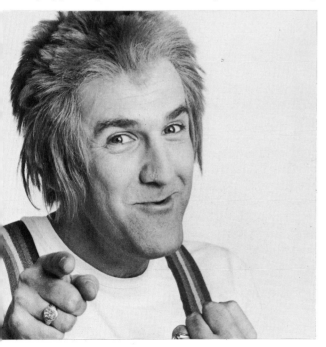

★ Russ Abbot says he has never been himself on stage. He finds his inspiration in costumes and props. 'I'm just myself until I put on a wig, then madness takes over' ★

ations, and in a 1985 *Lenny Henry Show* appeared as Michael Jackson (who shares Henry's birthday of 29 August 1958), Stevie Wonder, Prince and Tina Turner. 'She'd die for these legs,' he boasts. But he has gone on to create his own characters. The first was Algernon Spencer Churchill Gladstone Disraeli Palmerston Pitt the Younger Razzmatazz, who ate condensed milk sandwiches, but has since been discarded as a stereotype black. Others have been Delbert Wilkins, fast-talking Brixton wide boy and pirate station disc jockey (who featured in a complete series), the Rev Nathaniel Westminster (known as the Rev Nat-West), the Rev Dental Virtue, preaching from an altar flanked by dazzling dollar signs, Theophilus P. Wildebeeste, an American soul singer with a studded cod-piece and underpants with the studs inside, Fred Dread, Minister for Caribbean Affairs and a member of the Reggae Party, veteran blues singer Low Down Finger Lickin' Dirty Hound Dog Smith, and Deakus, a grizzled West Indian employed by London Transport. 'There are wonderful old boys like Deakus sitting in every corner of every pub,' says Henry.

He made his straight acting debut in *Coast to Coast*, a BBC2 movie in which he starred as a disc jockey on the run from small-time crooks, and his American film debut in *The Suicide Club*, co-starring with Meriel Hemingway.

Lenworth Henry, 6 ft 3 in tall, was born in Dudley, West Midlands. His dynamic mother, Winifred, emigrated from Jamaica in the mid-Fifties to create a new life for her family in England. She worked in a hospital and a factory until she had enough money to rent a flat and bring over her husband and Lenny and his two older brothers and sisters. (His father died in 1977, having just seen the beginning of Henry's success.) 'We weren't poor,' he says. 'There was always enough to eat but it was a real struggle. I never had any pocket money. It took weeks for the soles of our shoes to be mended and we had holes in our clothes.

'I was never small but comedy, for me, was all about making my friends laugh and being a useful member of the gang. If you're firstly a black guy and secondly not particularly good at anything, you have to find some way of contributing to the group. Humour was my way of doing it. There were a few other black guys at school but they were only really acquaintances. The guys I hung out with were

white. We'd go to clubs together and they were my mates. I could always mimic people and I'd do *Deputy Dawg* or *The Flintstones* and get laughs. I watched Mike Yarwood especially. Whatever he did on his Saturday night TV I came in and did on Monday morning at school. I'd have a couple of new voices and a few jokes and I'd add impressions of our teachers and lecturers and I'd be doing command performances all day.'

He was first on stage in a local ballroom impersonating Elvis Presley singing *Jailhouse Rock*. He also did Groucho Marx and Max Bygraves impersonations. All were of whites, apart from an impression of Muhammad Ali.

In the years following his *New Faces* win, he made what he calls 'darkie jokes'. He says: 'I tried to get by on rolling eyes, weird noises and dumb jokes. Like, if I was sweating, I'd wipe my face, lick my hand and say, "It's chocolate."' Then he came under the influence of Dawn French, whom he married in 1984, and her Comic Strip colleagues. He took Richard Pryor and Eddie Murphy as role models. In 1982 he rewrote his act. He now complains about white comics such as one he saw point out two blacks in the front row of an audience and say, 'I'd better be careful tonight or I'll get a spear through my head', and one who said to him, 'I knew you were coming because I heard the drums.'

He sends up racist comics with lines like: 'Now for some biting racist satire. Why do white people have normal noses? So they can breathe.' He says, 'True black humour is using the language and characteristics of your roots to make people laugh.'

While working two shows a night in Blackpool in 1984 he found a tutor and studied O-level English literature and language. He has campaigned against drug abuse among the young, and on behalf of the Sickle Cell Society, and visited Ethiopia in 1987 to report on the plight of its people during the Comic Relief fund-raising show which he co-presented. Henry has matured but still manages to send up blacks and whites and amuse both.

Victoria Wood

The world of Victoria Wood is full of forlorn women with varicose veins and dropped wombs, wearing discontinued Playtex bras under their Crimplene, and drinking coffee in Kardomah cafes. They shop at Habitat and tear out Sunday colour supplement offers of a dozen porcelain thimbles and a cut-price nose job. 'Pretension, that's my main target,' she says. 'People laugh at what they recognise.' She has an accurate ear for the absurdities of everyday speech.

She does not like dresses, and wears skirts only when playing roles. 'When I first started I thought I had to wear a frock, which I borrowed from a friend,' she says. She now appears on television in her award-winning shows in loud suits with thin ties, or a striped blazer, a track suit and trainers.

She was born in 1953 in Prestwich, Lancs, but was brought up in Bury, the daughter of an insurance underwriter, and took a drama degree at Birmingham University. She was working as a barmaid in Birmingham when she won *New Faces*. She went on to perform topical songs at the piano in Esther Rantzen's *That's Life*. One of the production team would telephone her on a Friday, draw her attention to a newspaper story, and ask her: 'Do something with that.' 'I could never write normal songs about love or anything,' she complains. 'I had to write songs about something that had happened, like the death of Guy the gorilla.'

In the second half of the Seventies her career stalled. No one seemed to want her any more. It was then that she found she could write sketches and plays as well as songs. *Talent*, a sad and funny play with songs, was about a sleazy Northern club where a plump girl (Wood) was supporting her glamorous friend (Julie Walters) at a talent contest. It won Wood an award as the

Most Promising Playwright of 1979, and she bought herself a frock (in a fat frock shop, she says) for the ceremony.

Wood and Walters had first met at the Manchester Polytechnic School of Theatre when Wood auditioned for a place, which she did not get, and was shown round by Walters who was a student there. Their partnership continued in other plays and in the TV comedy series *Wood and Walters* in 1980, which led to *Victoria Wood, As Seen on TV*. Walters also appeared in that, notably in wrinkled stockings as the doddering tea lady, Mrs Overall, in *Acorn Antiques*, a spoof of soap operas. Wood, a skilled interpreter of her own material, appeared with Patricia Routledge as Joan and Margery, presenters of household hints in an afternoon series, and other regulars in the shows included Susie Blake as an announcer: 'We'd like to apologise to viewers in the North. It must be *awful* for you.'

Wood writes all the words and all the songs for her shows, spending half the year writing in Morecambe, where she lives with her husband, Geoffrey Durham, who performs as the Great Soprendo, a Spanish magician. 'It is a very lonely life. I sit at my desk gazing out at sheep and cows, talking to nobody,' she says.

★ *Victoria Wood – as Seen on TV*. And she is only seen in a dress when in one of the television sketches she writes. For her stand-up performances she prefers a loud, baggy suit ★

Jim Davidson

Brash Cockney comic Jim Davidson won *New Faces* in 1976. Next day he went into the Dun Cow pub in the Old Kent Road – 'to see if anyone asked for my autograph' – and found the lunchtime comic had not arrived. Davidson did the show.

He was born in 1953 in a Blackheath council house, which he later bought for his parents. His father was a lorry driver, his mother worked as cleaner in a police station, and was later a cook in a factory canteen. He was the youngest of five, was christened Cameron and is still called Cam at home. He went to school in Charlton, but frequently cut lessons to go fishing, which is still a hobby.

'The show business thing started when I was 12,' he says. 'I went on holiday with my parents to Norfolk, where my father met a guy who was a friend of Ralph Reader and had connections with the London *Gang Show*. He asked me if I would like to audition for a spot on the show and I did the audition at the London Palladium and got the job. At that time I used to do a lot of impressions, so besides appearing in the 1966 *Gang Show* as part of the chorus I was given my very own six-minute spot. A star at 12! I also appeared in the following year's show and then I got totally disillusioned with show business after failing the audition for the part of the Artful Dodger in the film *Oliver!* That's it, I thought, I'm finished with the business. I was 14.'

He was a messenger boy, painter, window cleaner and van driver. 'I kept getting the sack,' he says. 'I couldn't get up in the morning and I was always late for work. I suppose I must have gone through three jobs a month. People got fed up with me. At 16 I used to play drums in a local pub – nothing special, just me and a piano player. Then one Sunday evening I went along to this pub in Woolwich where they had a regular stand-up comic appearing. On that particular night the comedian didn't turn up so, pushed into it by my friends, I ended up on stage telling gags and I got a great reception. About six months later a friend of mine rang me up and told me that the landlord of the Black Bull pub in Lewisham was looking for a comedian, so I nipped along there smartish and

★ A star at 12, fallen star at 14; the life of Cockney Jim Davidson has had its ups and downs ★

spun the guv'nor a right line about all the places I'd appeared in. He bought it and gave me the job at £6 a spot.'

His mother ironed his satin shirt and polished his shoes. 'There were a couple of coloured people and half a dozen of my mates,' he recalls. 'I wasn't getting any laughs until I started telling coloured jokes, then all the coloured blokes started falling about. Afterwards my mother used to ring pubs and clubs pretending to be an agent and offering this young comedian. I was soon making a good living from the business on a semi-pro basis. After my last normal job had folded I just lived off my earnings as a comedian.'

In the same year he won *New Faces* he starred in pantomime in Birmingham and broke the world non-stop joke-cracking record, which had been set at 5 hours 16 minutes by a Kansas comic. Davidson did 5 hours 22 mins 56 seconds without repeating himself, standing outside Longfield Park Hospital in Surrey. He finished drenched in perspiration, then raced to Brighton for two shows. 'When I changed my shirt its pattern was all over me vest,' he says.

He has become known for jokes about the police, and his 'nick nick' catch phrase. 'Nick nick wasn't original,' he says. 'Kids shouted it down our way when a copper appeared.' It has brought him many invitations to police smokers at which he often begins: 'Are there any policemen in the place? Or is that question too difficult?' He says: 'The CID love me to have a go at the uniformed branch and vice versa. They boo and cheer like kids.'

He later moved into TV situation comedy – unusually for a stand-up comic – in *Up the Elephant and Round the Castle* as a Cockney Jack-the-lad bequeathed a dilapidated house, and *Home James* as a chauffeur. He has been three times to the Falklands to entertain British troops and says: 'My pet hobby is history and I'm now expert on that war. People phone me up – soldiers and the Navy – and say, "When my ship was down there, what happened then?" and I tell them all about it.' He applied to go on *Mastermind* to answer questions on the Falklands war but abandoned the idea when he found he had to offer a second specialised subject in case he reached the final rounds. His three failed marriages and his numerous girlfriends have caused the tabloids to nickname him 'the Casanova comic'.

THE OXBRIDGE REVOLUTION

★

In the Sixties comedy underwent a series of revolutions after *Beyond the Fringe*, an Edinburgh Festival hit of 1960, arrived in London's West End the following year with Cambridge graduates Peter Cook and Jonathan Miller, and Oxford graduates Dudley Moore and Alan Bennett. Previously revues had been a cosy mix of Noel Coward style sketches and witty songs. The *Beyond the Fringe* crowd broke with tradition, sending up what they detested, and what they detested was what the Establishment revered: judges, policemen, vicars, war heroes, politicians, royals. Some people walked out of performances.

In the same year Cook and Nicholas Luard opened The Establishment, London's first satirical nightclub, with John Bird, John Fortune and Eleanor Bron, who had all been at Cambridge in the late Fifties with Cook and Luard. *Private Eye* began in the same year, and Cook was a founder of that too.

The BBC satire era followed in 1962 with *That Was the Week That Was*, establishing new comedy stars in presenter David Frost, William Rushton, John Wells, Millicent Martin and Roy Kinnear. It introduced a bite to television humour by enlisting writers from beyond the normal range of gag compilers. Playwrights, novelists and journalists contributed material that was sometimes juvenile, often savage. Targets included named politicians and businessmen. A profile of Home Secretary Henry Brooke, who had made controversial decisions about granting political asylum, described him as 'the most hated man in Britain' and ended, 'If you're Home Secretary you can get away with murder.' Frost would follow such an attack with the line: 'Seriously though, he's doing a grand job.'

Other taboos were ended. The Church could be mocked and one item which caused offence was a *Which?*-style consumer's guide to relig-ions. 'The Church of England,' it ran, 'is a jolly friendly faith....' A sketch written by Keith Waterhouse and Willis Hall showed two viewers (Roy Kinnear and Millicent Martin) staring at a TV set. 'Obscenity. It's all the go nowadays,' he said. 'You can say "bum", you say "po", you can say anything.' She retorted, 'You dirty devil!'

TW3 was transmitted live and director Ned Sherrin allowed cameras, boom microphones and stage hands to be seen. It was made by the current affairs department rather than by light entertainment, and mixed comic and serious. From four million viewers at the start its audience rose to 12 million, and this for a late night show which continued until midnight.

TW3 was axed at the end of 1963 on the grounds that 1964 was an election year, but resurfaced after the election as *Not So Much a Programme, More a Way of Life*, also hosted by Frost. This ran on all three nights of the weekend, with items including an operatic version of Edward the Eighth's abdication and a skit in which a Liverpool priest urged a working-class woman to have more children. Mary Whitehouse hated it and was not alone. William Shepherd, MP for Cheadle, attacked the BBC in a Commons debate complaining that in the previous week's show Lance Percival, dressed as Father Christmas, sang a song in which he referred to children as 'little bleeders'.

David Frost

Sherrin had engaged Frost after reading in *The Stage* of a new young Cambridge comic at the Blue Angel nightclub, who conducted an

★ *At Last the 1948 Show* (in 1967) with Aimi Macdonald, Tim Brooke-Taylor, John Cleese, Graham Chapman and Marty Feldman ★

★ 'Hello, good evening and welcome.'
Apart from performing comic routines
himself, David Frost has brought to the
screen many other performers ★

improvised press conference as Harold
Macmillan. Sherrin saw him doing the act and
hired him for TW3. His influence on comedy
was to be considerable.

David Paradine Frost, son of a Methodist
minister, was born in 1939 in Tenterden, Kent,
read English at Cambridge, and was secretary
of *Footlights*, the university revue. He had a
classless accent and a strange haircut. He began
in television in 1960 as a reporter in Norwich
for Anglia Television's regional news programme, for which his first recorded interview
was with two Cambridge councillors about a
plan to build shops, but executives felt he had
no future in regional broadcasting and his
contract was not renewed. In 1963 Frost
became a regular in an American version of
TW3, and began his commuting across the
Atlantic. He went on to star in *The Frost Report*
and *Frost Over England*, which once contrived to
show Prime Minister Harold Wilson and
Foreign Secretary George Brown apparently
dancing a jig, by running news clips forwards
and backwards.

At the end of the Sixties Frost was starring in
three weekend programmes on ITV. *Frost on
Friday* was a discussion show, *Frost on Saturday* an
interview show, *Frost on Sunday* a comedy show.
He also continued to make programmes in
America and was commuting 200,000 miles a
year. In his discussion programmes he scourged
fraudster Emil Savundra and drug doctor John
Peto. In his entertainment programmes he
presented an Old Testament newscast which
included a police message asking for information about Lot's wife, and ended with a
weather forecast: 'Egypt. A plague of locusts is
expected to sweep up from the south-west.
Sorry about that, Egypt.'

A founder of London Weekend Television
and of TV-am, he has also presented *Guinness
Book of Records* specials and the game show,
Through the Keyhole, and conducted scoop
interviews with President Nixon after Watergate
and the Shah of Iran in exile.

Peter Cook and Dudley Moore

The character of E.L. Wisty was introduced by
Peter Cook in the Cambridge University's
Footlight Revue of 1959. Wisty was originally a
miner who wanted to be a judge. Wisty then
appeared in *Beyond the Fringe*: 'God didn't just
say, "Let's have some coal", as he could have
done. He had all the right contacts. No, he got
this great wind going, you see, and blew down
all the trees, then over a period of three million
years he changed it into coal. It was all part of
the scheme but people at the time did not see it
that way. People under the trees did not say,
"Hurrah, coal in three million years." No, they
said "Oh dear, oh dear. Trees falling on us.
That's the last thing we want." And of course
their wish was granted.'

Cook has told me: 'I used to ad lib, changing
what I said regularly. I must have done 50
different Wisty pieces during my three years in
the show.' In ITV's *On the Braden Beat* Wisty
appeared weekly as President of the World
Domination League – slogan 'World
Domination by 1958'. (The series was seen in
1964.) Wisty was seated on a park bench in a
shabby raincoat and hat and stared un-
blinkingly at the camera. In *On the Braden Beat*
Wisty made no reference to life as a miner.
Cook told me at the time: 'I think now that
perhaps he never was a miner. I see him as a
lonely man, living in one room in Camberwell

★ *Beyond the Fringe* stars Peter Cook and Dudley Moore went on to create an outstanding comedy partnership in 1965 in the television series *Not Only . . . But Also* ★

but I don't know much about him. I don't even know what the initials EL stand for. I have never worked out a background for him. I just let him develop.'

Cook did not accept that Wisty was mad: 'A bit paranoic, of course, for he has delusions of grandeur, pride and persecution. And he is obsessed by power. He feels he is persecuted by spies, wasps and officials of all kinds.'

Each Saturday's spot was conceived on the previous Wednesday evening when Cook ad-libbed seven minutes of Wistyisms into a tape recorder. The following morning he played back the tape, pruned weaker passages and typed the script. 'The letters I get are surprising. Once I had 22 letters from a girls' school. Very romantic they were, too. But the biggest fan mail has concerned Spotty Muldoon.' (Spotty was Wisty's unseen friend, described by Wisty as being so pimply that he wore a paper bag over his head.) Cook also received postal orders with letters applying for membership of the World Domination League. 'I send them back, of course,' he said. 'Without explanation. How can I explain Wisty?'

Cook, whose father was in the Colonial service, went on to appear in a partnership with Dudley Moore, a railway electrician's son from Dagenham, who won an organ scholarship to Oxford. After *Beyond the Fringe* Moore

was playing with his own jazz trio at the Establishment Club when the BBC invited him to star in a programme. He invited Cook to be his guest and Cook wrote a sketch about two cloth-capped idiots, Dud and Pete. They went on to feature in a series, *Not Only . . . But Also,* in 1965. 'Funny!' Dud would say in response to some piece of misinformation from Pete. Other sketches written by Cook for the series included a classic in which Moore, as a one-legged man, pleaded with Cook as a film producer, for a Tarzan-type role. Each show began with a filmed version of the signature tune which Moore played in different surroundings, including Tower Bridge. The closing number was *Goodbye*, which got into the charts.

At the time I talked to Moore about the partnership amid hardboard tombstones in a field where he was on location for a film, he had just bought a 165 mph Maserati, with a refrigerator in the boot for keeping champagne cool. Moore, who said he thought he was 5 ft 3 in tall, insisted: 'I don't really worry about my height today, or that the difference in height between Peter Cook and myself gets such a laugh when we take a curtain. We didn't begin working together because of this. We found out after we had started that people found the difference in our heights so comic.'

Moore later moved to California to star with Bo Derek in the movie *10* and with Liza Minnelli in *Arthur*, and became nicknamed the Sex Thimble.

Monty Python

The greatest TV comedy hit of the Sixties came right at the end of the decade. John Cleese and Graham Chapman were Cambridge graduates who had appeared in ITV's *At Last the 1948 Show* in 1967. Michael Palin, Terry Jones and Eric Idle were Oxford graduates who starred in an ITV's children's comedy series, *Do Not Adjust Your Set*, in 1968. They had all written for, or appeared in, *The Frost Report*. They came together to make a comedy series for the BBC. The first proposed title was *Owl Stretching Time*; the second was *A Horse, a Spoon and a Basin*, but when it reached the screen in 1969 it was *Monty Python's Flying Circus*.

It was a mad half-hour involving upper-class twits, bumbling police, idiotic farmers and lecherous marriage counsellors. Regular characters included Michael Palin as gum-booted Mr Gumby, wearing a knotted handkerchief on his head and complaining his brain hurt. Eric Idle appeared asking oleaginously, 'Is your wife a goer then, eh, eh?' and when this brought him a cold stare, putting his finger alongside his nose and saying knowingly, 'Wink-wink, nudge-nudge, say no more.'

It sent up boring talk shows, pretentious TV documentaries and idiotic game shows. It introduced the Ministry of Silly Walks, Hell's Grannies, the Church Police, the Spanish Inquisition and a blancmange winning a tennis tournament. Nazi leaders reappeared in an English boarding house, a Confuse-a-Cat programme was devised to bring interest into the lives of bored pets. Among many sketches which have become classics was *The Parrot*, first seen in December 1969, with Cleese walking into a shop carrying a parrot in a cage. He complained it was dead, but Michael Palin as the shopkeeper tried to insist it was merely pining. 'It's not pining,' said the exasperated Cleese, 'it's passed on. This parrot is no more. It's ceased to be. It's expired. It's gone to meet its maker. This is a late parrot. It's a stiff. Bereft of life, it rests in peace. . . . It's an ex-parrot.'

A lecture on parts of the body introduced the expression 'naughty bits'. A voice over a sketch showing two men taking a bath said: 'They washed their arms, their legs and then they washed their naughty bits.' When it was shown in America in 1975 at 11.30 pm the sensitivities of the network censors caused them to bleep those two words.

The format was anarchic. Not all jokes had punchlines. A sketch would be terminated by Graham Chapman in army officer's uniform, declaring: 'This sketch is becoming silly. Stop it.' Upon which Cleese would announce: 'And now for something completely different.' Sometimes that was an animated cartoon sequence arranged by Terry Gilliam, an American, who was the one non-speaking member of the team.

During the last two years of the series there were personality clashes among the stars, some of whom thought the shows were less funny, others that they were funnier. *Python* ended in 1974, though the cast continued to get together on films including *Monty Python and The Holy Grail* and *Monty Python's Life of Brian* in the Seventies and *Monty Python's The Meaning of Life* in 1983.

John Cleese

Python's biggest star, in every sense, was 6 ft 5 in tall John Cleese, who generally played bowler-hatted figures of authority, hurling all the words of abuse to be found in a thesaurus. As an architect refused permission for an apartment-cum-abattoir block, he raged: 'This is just the kind of blinkered, philistine pig-ignorance I've come to expect from you non-creative garbage. You sit there on your loathsome, spotty behinds, squeezing blackheads, not caring a tinker's cuss for the struggling artist, you excrement, you whining, hypocritical toadies.'

American comedian Steve Martin has called Cleese the funniest man in the world. He was born in 1939 in Weston-super-Mare where his father sold insurance. He was an only child and 6 ft tall at the age of 12. 'I spent a lot of time on my own, playing on my own and being quite content to do so,' he says. 'When I was suddenly shoved into forms of 20 people I had difficulty in being accepted until I discovered that I could make them laugh.'

He went to Cambridge to read law, and joined *Footlights* just as Peter Cook and David Frost were leaving; two years later he starred in the *Footlights* revue, *Cambridge Circus*, which later ran in London West End and New York, where he met Connie Booth, an American actress who was working as a waitress. They were married, and together wrote the series *Fawlty Towers* in 1975. It was set in a terrible West Country hotel based on one in Torquay at which they had stayed. The owner rebuked one guest for using his knife and fork in the American manner – the guest was, in fact, American – and threw another's guest's briefcase out of the hotel, declaring that it probably contained a bomb. Cleese maintains: 'The owner was the most wonderfully rude man I've ever met. He maintained the guests stopped him from running his hotel.'

Cleese played the manic, blustering Basil Fawlty, Prunella Scales his domineering wife Sybil, and Connie Booth the pert maid, Polly, the most sensible person in the hotel – sometimes, it seemed, the only one. Andrew Sachs played Spanish waiter Manuel, the butt of Fawlty's bullying, whose invariable response to any instruction was 'Que?', whereupon Fawlty would explain to guests: 'You'll have to excuse him – he comes from Barcelona.' It was one of the briefest of successful sitcoms – only 13 episodes were made.

A shy, uptight man, Cleese claims to have become calmer, quieter and more tolerant after undergoing therapy. A company which he founded to make management training films had already made him wealthy; the phenomenal success of the film, *A Fish Called Wanda,* which he wrote and starred in as a silver-tongued barrister in 1988, seemed set to make him a millionaire.

★ **John Cleese (far left) in** *Monty Python* **and right as Basil Fawlty** ★

★

THE GRADUATES II

★

The Seventies brought two more waves of graduate entertainers to television. The first consisted of others who had been students at Cambridge at the same time as John Cleese and, like him, emerged in the revue *Cambridge Circus*, a success in the West End and on Broadway. One sketch in it had men in pinstripes on a Green Line bus bursting into a negro spiritual. 'Everyone assumed that because we were undergrads it must be satire but we were positively reacting against it,' says Bill Oddie, who came to television in *The Goodies* with Tim Brooke-Taylor and Graeme Garden.

The Goodies

The Goodies started on BBC television in 1973, were almost as anarchic as *Python* and often more visual, one of their classics being a sequence in which mechanical excavators were seen snapping and savaging like prehistoric monsters. Another showed low-flying geese dropping golden eggs that skipped towards their target like the bouncing bombs of the RAF's Dam Busters. In another sketch the Queen offered the hand of the Prince of Wales to the person who could rid the country of a plague of Rolf Harrises. Executives were worried about offending the royals, so Brooke-Taylor grabbed an opportunity to relate the plot to the Prince. 'Far from being upset, he thought it was a great joke and seriously pressed us to let him play himself in the scene,' he says. 'However, it was eventually thought it might be a little undignified for the future King and we went ahead using photographic studies of the Prince. I was the "bride".'

Brooke-Taylor, from Buxton, Derbyshire, read law at Cambridge. He was known as 'Timbo' in the *Goodies* and wore a Union Jack waistcoat. Sometimes the absurdity of the way he earns a living overwhelms him. 'There are

moments,' he says, 'when I'm standing in the middle of some High Street dressed as a rabbit and I say to myself, "I've not only got a degree but I'm a Doctor of Laws. *Doctor* Tim Brooke-Taylor. What am I doing hopping down this High Street in floppy ears and a furry tail?"'

For a medieval vasectomy sketch filmed in a park outside London he had to stand back to camera, trousers around ankles while a knight on a charger rushed him with lance aimed at a sensitive area. In other programmes he has also suffered indignities. In *Me and My Girl* with Richard O'Sullivan, he appeared as a turkey and in *Assaulted Nuts* he had to go into a shop and whip off his coat to reveal frilly French knickers and suspenders. 'I wanted the set cleared when we were filming it so that I'd look a complete fool in front of as few people as possible,' he says.

'It didn't seem to make any sense that I should become a comedian but I found it wasn't just a question of making the money. I found a great satisfaction in making people happy.'

Rochdale-born Bill Oddie, who read English at Cambridge, wrote a large part of *Cambridge Circus* as well as playing in it, but got into student show business through music. He could not write music, or play any instrument at the time (though he later played drums), but he could compose pastiche rock'n'roll using a tape recorder. He went on to be the musical member of the Goodies, creating such numbers as *Funky Gibbon* (a hit in 1975), *Black Pudding Bertha*, *Nappy Love* and *Make a Daft Noise for Christmas*.

Today he is best known as an expert on bird watching, a hobby of his since he was a teenager

★ 'We think in terms of a human animated cartoon,' said Tim Brooke-Taylor of *The Goodies*, in which he starred with the moustached Bill Oddie and Graeme Garden ★

when his ambition was to be a warden of a bird sanctuary.

Graeme Garden, referred to in *The Goodies* as 'Old Graybags', is a doctor's son from Aberdeen, now a doctor himself. Since *The Goodies* he has moved into popularising medical matters on TV. In the first programme of the BBC's *Bodymatters*, which aimed to reveal basic facts about the human body with giant working models and parlour games, he was hung upside down, 'just so that people at home could see me right way up pouring champagne upwards'. That was to help explain how the eyes work. In another programme in the series he suffered himself to be picked up by strong man Geoff Capes, 'to perch like a parrot on his biceps'.

Not the Nine O'Clock News
At the end of the Seventies came another wave of graduate entertainers. In 1979 the BBC, in its wisdom, entrusted the task of producing a new TV comedy series to John Lloyd, who was working in radio, and Sean Hardie, who was a *Panorama* producer and had never made a comedy show. Both had studied at Trinity College, Cambridge, but Lloyd read law and Hardie read history and they never met.

They needed a cast and the first choice was Rowan Atkinson who, although an Oxford man, they knew because he had also worked in radio production. 'Rowan was the only obvious one,' said Lloyd. 'Everyone knew he was going to be incredibly famous. It was a question of who got him first.'

Then they thought of Griff Rhys Jones because Lloyd had been with him in the 1973 *Footlights Revue*, and Mel Smith because Jones and Lloyd had been to Oxford to see the rival annual revue and he had made them laugh. The fourth member of the team was Pamela Stephenson, spotted by Lloyd at a lunch party. 'She was the most attractive girl there and I got to talk to her,' he says. 'We hadn't cast an actress at that stage and I found her very amusing.'

Rowan Atkinson
Rowan Atkinson has eyes like gob stoppers and lips like putty. He says his face has 'a malleable nature'. Others describe him as rubber-faced or like a *Spitting Image* puppet. His face has certainly been responsible in part for his success, though he also has an incisive voice,

superb timing and projects a streak of cruelty.

Some comics struggle for years to reach the top, but everything has gone his way. He was born in 1955 in Newcastle-upon-Tyne, where his father was a businessman and farmer. His older brothers are a merchant banker and a steel exporter. His first recollection of making people laugh goes back to when he was 11 and used to jump up and down in the school changing room, pulling faces. 'Once heard, the sound of laughter appealed to me and although it was never my intention to make acting a career there was always an awareness of just how much I liked performing,' he says. Eventually, his headmaster called him into his office and said that although he had never before recommended a pupil to enter show business he would not disapprove if Atkinson gave it a try.

First, however, he read electrical engineering at Newcastle for his BSc and went on to Oxford for a Master's degree in electronics. It was there he decided finally on show business. He made his London debut in 1977 at Hampstead in a revue, *Beyond a Joke*, with a slightly sinister routine as a schoolmaster reading the class register: 'Ainsley . . . Babcock . . . . Carthorse . . . Dirt . . . Elsworth-Beast Major . . . Elsworth-Beast Minor . . . Fiat . . . Kosygin . . . Nibble . . . Plectrum . . . Orifice . . . Undermanager.'

He then wrote and appeared in a situation comedy for LWT which was screened in 1979 under the flattering title, *Rowan Atkinson Presents – Canned Laughter*, but declined to follow it with a series in order to join the *Not the Nine O'Clock News* team. He was making that series within nine months of leaving university and, after only 21 editions of it, opened in his first one-man show, the youngest person to have such a show in the West End. In 1980 he won a Variety Club award as BBC Personality of the Year.

He has since starred in the medieval comedy, *The Black Adder*, followed by *Blackadder II, III* and *IV*, playing, among other Blackadders, a courtier of Queen Elizabeth the First and butler to the Prince Regent. His hobby is driving heavy goods vehicles. 'I think I'm rather lonely as a person and I like the idea of being up there in a cab all by myself,' he says. 'Maybe I could run a theatrical trucking company.'

Smith and Jones

Mel Smith and Griff Rhys Jones had met briefly as students when Smith was directing student drama at Oxford and Jones was doing the same thing at Cambridge. Smith's father owned a betting shop in Chiswick and Smith grew up over the shop – despite this, he was once practically a full-time gambler. At Oxford he read experimental psychology but after graduating carried on directing at theatres in Bristol, Sheffield and London. He was six years in the West End before ever stepping in front of an audience.

While Atkinson was identified as the funny one, Smith as the fat one, and Stephenson as the sexy one, Jones was the one whose name no one could remember. The son of a doctor and a nurse, he went to Cambridge to read history and English literature. After graduating he was for a time a minder to Arabs visiting London. He was introduced to this by a university

★ Rowan Atkinson, above, and Mel Smith and Griff Rhys Jones, left, established themselves in *Not the Nine O'Clock News* in 1979. Atkinson went on to be acclaimed in various series of *Blackadder* ★

★ Mel Smith and Griff Rhys Jones teamed up after *Not the Nine O'Clock News*, and worked together in many series including *The World According to Smith and Jones* in which they provided a commentary linked to old film clips ★

friend, Douglas Adams, author of *Hitch-hiker's Guide to the Galaxy*. 'There was nothing dangerous about it,' he says. 'We sat outside hotel rooms for 12 hours at a stretch and kept the dignitaries from being bothered.' Then he became a BBC radio producer working on *Top of the Form* and with Frankie Howerd and Alfred Marks.

Jones is all high voltage, a worrier who talks at hurricane speed, makes jokes and pulls faces. Smith is relaxed. However, they became close friends while making *Not the Nine O'Clock News* and went on to star together in *Alas Smith and Jones* in which they developed their head to head dialogues shot in close up. 'Basically two idiots talking,' says Mel. 'They're both stupid but one of them pretends he isn't.'

In one programme Smith tried to explain to Jones about sperm bank donorship. Jones asked: 'Do you have the lights out there? When you're....'

Smith: 'No, no, there's no need to have the lights out. There's nobody there but you.'

Jones: 'Well, where is this woman, then, while you're....'

Smith: 'Don't know. Might be anywhere. Probably shopping.'

In another, talking about recording stars, Smith said: 'Take Buddy Holly, for instance.'

Jones: 'Buddy Holly? He reminds me of an assistant bank manager in his glasses and that.'

Smith: 'Rubbish. Buddy was one of the greats. He was a genius. He was ... on a different plane.'

Jones: 'I bet he wishes he had been.'

The two also wrote and starred together in their first film, *Morons from Outer Space*, about aliens landing on the M1 amid smoke, sparks and pile-ups. It was a disaster. They starred together in ITV's *The World According to Smith and Jones*, commentating on clips from old films. They have also formed a company called Talkback, which produces radio and TV commercials. Separately, Jones has appeared on stage in *Charley's Aunt* and in lager commercials, co-starring by means of clever editing with John Wayne, Barbara Stanwyck, James Cagney and others in scenes from old movies, while Smith has played a councillor on the make in ITV's *Muck and Brass* and starred in the West End in *Gambler*, a play he wrote himself.

Pamela Stephenson

Pamela Stephenson, the one girl in *Not the Nine O'Clock News*, was noted for her cutting impersonations of Angela Rippon, Jan Leeming, Sue Lawley and Kate Bush. A tiny blonde, she was born in 1950 in Auckland, New Zealand, the daughter of two scientists, but grew up in Australia. She dropped out of university and trained at the Australian National Institute of Dramatic Art, then followed the hippie trail, hitch-hiking around the Far East and Eastern Europe before arriving, broke, in London in 1976 to become an actress. She appeared in small glamour parts in series including *The New Avengers, Space 1999* and the private eye series, *Hazell*, after which she married its star, Nicholas Ball.

Her appearance has been eye-catching – her hair white with pink and green highlights, diamanté aircraft on her ears and crazy spectacles on her nose. She has worn rainbow-hued jackets, turquoise trousers and pink stilettos. She has been described as looking like an exotic tropical bird with ruffled plumage, though her own assessment was 'like a coloured feather duster'.

Her behaviour has shocked. On TV-am she tried to debag presenter Nick Owen and threw raw eggs about. On a Bob Monkhouse chat show she fired a revolver. On a Michael Parkinson show she entwined her thighs around Reginald Bosanquet's neck. At a Woman of the Year lunch at the Savoy, attended by Princess Michael of Kent, she told a string of risqué jokes, and was reputed to have once stripped under a restaurant table. A critic who slated her appearance on stage in Gilbert and Sullivan's *The Pirates of Penzance* received a wrapped and boxed cowpat. In 1987 she stood for parliament as the 'Put a Blancmange Down Terry Wogan's Y-fronts' candidate for Windsor Maidenhead – for fun and because the *Wogan* show had cancelled an appearance by her. She polled 328 votes without campaigning.

Her one-woman shows have borne such titles as: *Small But Perfectly Formed* and *Naughty Night Nurses Without Panties Down Under No. 2*. In these shows she played as many as 28 parts including Ian Paisley, Arthur Scargill, Janet Street-Porter, a baby and Joan Collins as the Virgin Mary in a school nativity play. 'How many women here tonight have never faked an orgasm?' she would ask at the beginning, and go on to talk about oral sex and vibrators. Once she pulled giant plastic breasts from her jumpsuit and put them on her head, and to a heckler's cry of 'Getemoff', she would retort: 'Have that boy washed and brought to my tent.'

After the break-up of her marriage to Ball came her association with Billy Connolly. She settled down as a teetotal, non-smoking, vegetarian and mother of three, but was still capable of surprises. Before the wedding of Prince Andrew, while he and Connolly were at a stag party, she hired policewomen's uniforms for herself, the Princess of Wales and the about-to-be Duchess of York, and they went to Annabel's nightclub in them.

★ Pamela Stephenson looking demure – which has not always been the case. She has startled and shocked viewers in the past but has quietened since settling down with Billy Connolly and becoming a mother ★

CREATING AN IMPRESSION

★

'**I**'m going to take you to a Hollywood party,' they used to say, and then with appropriate props would impersonate Maurice Chevalier, James Cagney, Humphrey Bogart and James Stewart. A girl would don a felt hat and growl, 'I vant to be alone', and would be applauded as Garbo. Mike Yarwood changed all that and took impressions into a new era.

Mike Yarwood

Yarwood also impersonated stars, but mainly contemporary ones from other TV shows, and he ranged far beyond them. He was doing Harold Macmillan, Lord Boothby and Malcolm Muggeridge when other people were doing Edward G. Robinson and Peter Lorre. He impersonated sportsmen and trade union leaders, politicians and members of the royal family, and he did not merely impersonate them. He used them as characters, casting them in improbable situations in which they impersonated each other, embarked on new careers or took part in cross-talk acts. His Harold Wilson, pipe between teeth, told Edward Heath: 'When you die, Ted, I'm going to dance on your grave,' and his Heath, shoulders shaking with mirth, retorted: 'Good, I'm going to be buried at sea.'

At a reception at Buckingham Palace for a charity organisation, Prince Charles told him: 'I hope you're not going to start doing me.' Yarwood was not sure whether it was a warning or an invitation, but it put the idea into his head and he did him.

Harold Wilson (now Lord Wilson) has said: 'As far afield as the Isles of Scilly the first thing a lot of people ask me about is Mike Yarwood's impersonations. It's something of a chore to have people coming up to me and saying, "It *is* Mike Yarwood, isn't it?", especially when you've had it five times in the last 10 minutes.' No one was a someone until impersonated by

Yarwood. Neil Kinnock said, 'Being done by Mike is one of the perks of my job. I only wish I had as much hair.'

Yarwood introduced lines that became catch phrases and which most viewers believe were said by the subjects of the impressions, although often they were entirely the work of Yarwood and his writers. Hughie Green's 'I mean that most sincerely, friends', Max Bygraves's hand-flapping 'I wanna tell you a story', and Denis Healey's references to people as 'silly billies' were not said by them – or at least, not until after Yarwood had put the lines in their mouths.

Asked his favourite characters, he usually named whichever politician was latest in his repertoire, and Dave Allen – 'because he's got lots of mannerisms and because I can sit down'. Dave Allen responded to Yarwood's impression of him by sitting on his stool, languidly brushing imaginary specks off his trousers, as Yarwood had done, and then asking the studio audience, 'Doesn't that Mike Yarwood fidget?'

Yarwood claims he has never worried about people taking offence because he has never been cruel, and Lord Wilson agrees: 'There's no malice in him at all; he's not trying to send you up in a destructive way.' The only star Yarwood has ever offended, so far as he knows, is Frankie Howerd, who thought an impression made him seem effeminate. However, Yarwood finds it difficult to assess reactions. 'The only person who has ever complimented me is Harold Wilson,' he says. 'James Callaghan told me I hadn't got him right because I wasn't tall enough, which is quite true, and I got the impression from Edward Heath that he didn't know I'd done him; I don't think he watches

★ No, it is not Boy George but Les Dennis impersonating Boy George. The impression is remarkable, though Dennis says singing is not his strong point ★

much television. The majority of people I impersonate come up to say thank you, but they don't actually comment. The truth is, people rarely see themselves the way others do, or the way they really are. They're not aware of their mannerisms.'

Life became less easy for him when Margaret Thatcher became Prime Minister. He said his face was too pudgy for him to impersonate her. 'Ena Sharples is about the only woman I've been able to mimic successfully,' he says.

His normal method of working was to videotape potential victims off TV for about a minute – 'Just enough to go on. I can hear voices in my head and in my mind so I don't play the tapes over and over. I watch my subjects once or twice and if I don't get them very quickly, almost instinctively, I don't get them at all.' He says impressions are a knack. 'Kids often write to me and ask, "How do I become a mimic?" But you don't become one. You've either got the gift or you haven't. Most people can do at least one impression, but to be able to do different impressions, to have a repertoire, is something else.'

One curiosity of the Yarwood performances is that while he could sing very competently as Sinatra and others, when he announced, 'And this is me', and returned to his own voice, the quality of his singing fell noticeably. He cannot explain this, but says he is also funnier as Ken Dodd or another comic than as himself. Always a worrier, Yarwood regards himself as dull when being himself. 'Performing is an escape from shyness,' he says.

He was born in 1941 in Bredbury, Cheshire. 'Even as a child I was a mimic,' he says. 'I used to imitate the butcher, the milkman, the baker, the parish priest, and my mother used to get me to perform for the neighbours.' On his last day at school the head assembled teachers in the school library and Yarwood was summoned to perform for them. 'I went through them all one by one; they all laughed a lot except for the one I was actually impersonating at the time.'

He left school at 15 and at 18 was working for a mail order firm in Manchester as a dispatch clerk but was fired for impersonating the boss. He was then playing drums with an unsuccessful group, and impersonating Cliff Richard and Adam Faith. In a talent competition in a pub in Dukenfield he came third of the four contestants, but in the bar afterwards a publican

offered him a job in a Manchester pub – two spots on a Friday night for 30 shillings (£1.50). He bought hats in the styles favoured by Harry Worth, Tony Hancock and Wilfrid Brambell as Albert Steptoe and two weeks later he turned professional and began working Manchester clubs.

He first did Harold Wilson when he became Leader of the Opposition, and that led to a spot on *Sunday Night at the London Palladium*. 'Wilson is my version of a hit record,' he said once.

In 1982, after 11 years with the BBC, he moved to ITV for a bigger budget, but in the mid-Eighties he developed a drink problem, his marriage broke up and his ITV contract was not renewed. In 1988 he decided to switch to acting, and began a tour of the country in the farce, *One for the Pot*, but collapsed, suffering from exhaustion and had to pull out of his next engagement as Wishee Washee in the pantomime *Aladdin*. He was still trying to rebuild his career when this book was written.

Bobby Davro

Largely due to Yarwood, there was a vogue for impressions shows in the Seventies. *Who Do You Do?* featured a team of mimics in as many as 50 impressions in a programme. *Go For It* and *Copy Cats* in the Eighties created a new generation of impressionists, though all had one thing in common. Gary Wilmot says: 'Ask any impressionist and he will tell you he has always been able to mimic other people; I found out I could do it when I was at school and used to take off friends and teachers.' Allan Stewart says: 'When I was a kid I was always taking people off; my mother used to be horrified if I was ever near anyone with a twitch because she knew I wouldn't be able to resist taking him off.' A.J. Harvey says: 'I started out by taking the mickey out of the teachers at school, in Manchester – and usually got the cane for it.'

One of the most successful of the stars of *Copy Cats* was Bobby Davro, who went on to have his own shows, such as *Bobby Davro's Sketch Pad*. Davro has made a speciality of impersonating pop stars such as Elton John and George Michael, who went to see Davro in a show at Windsor. Davro says: 'George slipped into the show and I saw him squirming away in the audience as I took him off, but afterwards he came backstage and said he had really enjoyed the act. All I can say is that he must have been

★ Bobby Davro as Max Headroom, the flip, computer-generated android (played by Matt Frewer) who presented a pop video show of that name on Channel 4 in 1985 ★

blessed with a really good sense of humour.'

Davro does not see his impressions as being cruel, saying he nearly always impersonates artists of whom he is a fan. 'I agree some of my impressions are a bit wicked but comedy is based on that. Some of the artists I do who do not take it lightly should realise that it is not ridicule, it is a parody of their character. If I'm not happy with the way I'm portraying someone, then I just don't do it. I'm too much of a perfectionist.

'The very nature of the business makes you insecure and defenceless; there have been times when I've felt I cannot do another impression or take on any new characters – and that frightens me. It happens when I've been working really hard doing the same people and then have the challenge of taking on a new role.

I just have to take a deep breath and launch myself into long, arduous practice sessions. Once you build up a reputation of being funny you have to work hard to maintain it.'

He jokes about the police and well-built girls and ethnic groups. He says: 'When I do my stand up shows there are often Indians in the audience and I'll joke with them, saying, "What are you doing here? Who's minding the corner shop tonight?" They don't mind. They laugh along with everyone else.' However, his material has been described as racist and sexist by alternative comics who prefer comedy to be about topical issues. Davro is unapologetic. He says: 'Politics don't play a big part in my life so I tend to avoid political jokes. I'm neither right wing nor left wing. I don't really care. Do young people want to hear about politics all the time or do comedians think that's what audiences want?'

Davro was born in Ashford, Surrey, in 1958, the son of former Olympic miler Bill Nankeville. 'As a child I was a bit of a show-off,' he says. 'I loved taking the mickey out of people.' At 12 he impersonated comics such as Ken Goodwin. 'I aim for the voice first and then the facial features seem to come in.'

At 16 he started work in the men's department of a store in Kingston, Surrey, and impersonated John Inman in *Are You Being Served?* to amuse the staff. Later he imitated Humphrey Bogart, Harold Wilson and Michael Crawford's Frank Spencer in a talent contest and at 18 was touring as a professional entertainer. He took Davro as his stage name from his father's retail store which was named Davro after sons David and Robert (Bobby).

Les Dennis

Unusually in the impressions game, Les Dennis made his name in a double act. He teamed with Dustin Gee in 1982 and two years later they were starring on television in *The Laughter Show* and impersonating *Coronation Street*'s Mavis Wilton and Vera Duckworth. 'I don't really know,' said Dennis as Mavis, and it became a catch phrase, though she had never said it in *Coronation Street*. But in 1986 Gee collapsed from a heart attack when they were on stage together playing the Ugly Sisters in the pantomime *Cinderella*. He died three days later.

'I lost a friend as well as a partner, but you just have to get on with it,' said Dennis as he

★ Les Dennis found fame as half of a double act with Dustin Gee who died in 1986. Since then Dennis has worked solo. 'I go for the thumbnail caricature,' he says ★

working men's clubs where audiences were sympathetic because of his youth, though this did not extend outside. He was mugged on his way home from a club one night and displayed a black eye on stage next evening.

In 1987 he succeeded Max Bygraves as presenter of *Family Fortunes*.

Rory Bremner

Among all the new generation of impressionists the accolade of 'the new Mike Yarwood' has been awarded most often to Rory Bremner. It does not please him. 'It's just journalese, trying to put me in a category,' he says. 'For one thing I don't sing, though neither could he, except in character when he sang beautifully.' For another thing, he says, he always found Yarwood too cosy. Bremner likes to satirise rich, famous and politically right-wing targets including President George Bush and Denis Thatcher, as impersonated by John Wells. A favourite joke, delivered in the voice of newscaster Sandy Gall, is: 'And the man who propositioned Mrs Thatcher said he was sorry but he was only trying to do to her what's she's doing to the economy.'

His range is wider than that. In one show alone he did impersonations of Prince Charles, Dame Edna Everage, Jimmy Savile, Sir David Attenborough, Dennis Norden, Michael Foot, David Steel, Brian Walden, Tony Benn and Neil Kinnock. He likes Kinnock and impersonated him at one function where the Labour party leader was speaking. Other subjects have included Keith Floyd, Jonathan Miller, Russell Grant, Desmond Lynam, Roy Hattersley and Barry Norman.

'The real reason I do anything is for a laugh, but it's got to have a point,' he says. 'It's not enough to get up and do Frank Spencer. I like to say something about the character.' As Sir Robin Day he announces: 'Good evening and welcome, and again tonight we're pleased to welcome a token woman to *Question Time*.' The NHS, poll tax and the controversial TV documentary *Death on the Rock* have also received his treatment.

Bob Monkhouse was reputed to dislike his *Opportunity Knocks* spoof, *Sincerity Sucks*. On stage in *Comic Relief* in front of millions of viewers he was going from political reporter John Cole into Bob Monkhouse when his two false front teeth slipped in his mouth and he had

returned to work on his own in *The Les Dennis Laughter Show*, impersonating Paul Hogan, Esther Rantzen, Leslie Grantham (as Dirty Den in *Eastenders*), Bruce Willis and Frank Bough. 'I go for the thumbnail caricature,' he says of his act, in which he relies heavily on make up. 'Once you start to look like the person you're halfway there,' he says. Singing is not his strong point. 'I've got an ear for mimicry but I haven't got a musical ear,' he says. 'Obviously the two things are not connected at all. I can remember a tune but it just doesn't come out right.'

Dennis was born in 1954 in Liverpool. His father, Leslie Heseltine, was a former Liverpool soccer player turned bookie and his mother worked in a factory. He entered talent shows from the age of nine and came third in one at 10. He started his career at 14 in tough northern

★ The man most often hailed as 'the new Mike Yarwood' is Rory Bremner, though it is not a title he welcomes. He likes to satirise the rich and powerful ★

to ad-lib extra facial contortions and strangulated noises until he could get them back into position. 'Most of the viewers seemed to think it was my best Monkhouse impersonation,' he says dryly.

Bremner says he tries to strike a balance between the satirical and the funny. 'My satire's not always funny,' he admits. 'The satire is the pill and the comedy is the sugar.' Among the purely comic items was one in which he walked Eastbourne's main street dressed as Quentin Crisp, wearing a magenta wig, lipstick and long fingernails. 'I got such peculiar looks from people because they couldn't see the camera crew,' he says.

Edinburgh-born, tall and athletic with curly red hair, he is the son of an army officer, was educated at Wellington College, and took a degree in languages at King's College, London. He first attracted attention at the Edinburgh Festival when he was a student in 1981 and he was on the alternative cabaret circuit when the BBC put him into *Wogan* in 1985. A royal gala appearance followed, then his BBC series, *Now Something Else*, in 1986.

★

COMIC ACTORS

★

Most actors and actresses have in their time played comedy roles in sitcoms, and these have included some of the best, though there are those who look down on the genre. David Jason says: 'Sitcom is like the poor relation in showbiz. I don't see why. It's successful and the most watched sort of programme on television, yet the most maligned.' When Dame Judi Dench and her husband, Michael Williams, starred in ITV's gentle *A Fine Romance* in 1981 they told me that some of their peers had warned them that they were demeaning themselves. They were, however, hugely successful in it. Other actors and actresses specialise in sitcom, and have created comedy characters with which they have continued to be identified, sometimes to the extent of being referred to by their character names – although this rarely pleases them. The next two chapters are about some of these.

Harry H. Corbett and Wilfrid Brambell

Steptoe and Son was different from the run of domestic sitcoms in involving no married couple, no children, just two interdependent men, father and son. It was also different in that they were not comfortably middle class but rag and bone men, earning a meagre income from collecting scrap with a horse and cart, and living in squalid poverty. Albert was unshaven and toothless, a wheedling, cunning, sneering old man. His son, Harold, was a daydreamer, seeking to improve himself but always thwarted by the father he was unable to bring himself to leave, although he was past 40.

Steptoe and Son began as a one-off playlet, *The Offer*, in a series called *Comedy Playhouse* in 1962, and was written by Alan Simpson and Ray Galton after Tony Hancock had parted company with them. The name Steptoe was taken by them from the sign on a shop they had passed in a car: 'Steptoe and, by the Grace of God, his

Seven Sons Ltd'.

The roles were played by Wilfrid Brambell and Harry H. Corbett (who inserted the middle initial to distinguish himself from the creator of Sooty, and was known to friends as 'H'). Both Brambell, born in Dublin, and Corbett, a Londoner, were versatile and experienced actors, respected in the profession, but it was the first time they had worked together. When a series was proposed a year later Brambell turned it down for fear of becoming typecast, but the BBC increased the money and he accepted.

The characters they played had a love and hate relationship. Much of the time it was hate. 'You dirty old man,' Harold admonished his father, 'You idle old git.' To which Albert snarled: 'You can't wait to hear the first shovelful of dirt hit the coffin, can you?' On rare occasions they were sentimental. In *The Birthday* Harold gave Albert a pair of gloves and took him for a meal at a Chinese restaurant. Inevitably they quarrelled and Harold went home by car leaving the old man to take the Underground, where he lost the gloves and arrived home near to tears. Harold told him: 'Never mind, Dad, I'll get you another pair.'

Brambell's favourite episode was *The Holiday* in which Harold set his heart on going abroad for the first time, while the old man wanted to return to a boarding house in Bognor Regis. Albert then had a heart attack and they went to Bognor. Brambell's least favourite episode was one in which he was seen in a bath, eating pickled onions and dropping them in the

★ Two BBC situation comedies separated by a decade, but both of them television landmarks. *Steptoe and Son* starred Harry H. Corbett and Wilfrid Brambell in the Sixties. *Porridge* starred Ronnie Barker in the Seventies ★

bathwater. A fastidious man, he claimed that despite the most expensive bath salts and toiletary preparations he stank like an empty vinegar bottle for days afterwards.

Steptoe and Son began in 1964 and though it shocked many, it had eight million viewers weekly in 1965, including the Queen Mother who told Brambell she was a fan. There was a gathering of 400 Steptoes, many named Albert and Harold, at Woburn Abbey, which Brambell attended, though not Corbett, who was shy, and during the run of the series rarely went out without hat and glasses. People still asked him, 'How's the horse?' or 'How's the old man?' He protested: 'Harold is not me. I don't even know anything about him. He only exists on paper.'

The series ran until 1973 and America made a version, *Sanford and Son*. Corbett died in 1982 and Brambell in 1985.

Warren Mitchell

Till Death Us Do Part in 1966 had an even more unsavoury hero in Alf Garnett, bald, baggy-trousered, bigoted and ranting about race, religion and royalty. His moustache dripping with beer foam, he railed against those he called kikes, wogs, the bloody Irish and coons – 'stinking the country out with their curries and making a row with their dustbin lids'. He denounced rock'n'rolling vicars, sex maniacs and the Labour party. 'Labour lost the last election because Michael Foot went on telly promising to put four million back to work and frightened the life out of them.' He was for Christianity and the Queen: 'She should have her own series cos she's better'n Lulu; blimey, she's the best thing on at Christmas.'

'A rampaging, howling embodiment of all the most vulgar and odious prejudices that slop about in the bilges of the national mind,' wrote T.C. Worsley in the *Financial Times*. 'He is everything most hateful about our national character – xenophobic, illiberal, racist, anti-Semitic, toadying, authoritarian. He's a flogger, a censor, a know-all and a Mister-Always-Right. He is a positive anthology of unconsidered bigotry... The more outrageous and extreme his tirades grow, the more we adore him.'

Writer Johnny Speight drew Garnett as a grotesque caricature to lampoon prejudice, yet Garnett voiced opinions that could be heard in pubs and factories, and many viewers probably listened to his outpourings with approval.

Garnett lived in an East End slum house with an outside loo, and had a downtrodden wife, Else, played by Dandy Nichols. 'Silly moo', he called her, or 'yer great puddin'. Their daughter Rita (Una Stubbs) was shocked by his bigotry yet fond of him. His son-in-law, Mike

★ Sitcom heroes do not need to be likeable. Steptoe Senior was dirty. Alf Garnett, was a ranting, bigot ★

(Anthony Booth) was an idle left-winger whom Garnett addressed as 'Shirley Temple', because of his long hair, or 'Scouse git', because he came from Liverpool.

Alf Garnett divided the country. Clean-up TV campaigner Mary Whitehouse, counting six 'bloodies' and 'a number of dirty innu-endoes' in one programme thought he was a filthy, foul-mouthed brute. Yet within a year the BBC was claiming some 18 million viewers and there was an American version, *All in the Family*.

The series ran to 1974, with a sequel in 1985, *In Sickness and in Health*, in which Alf was pushing Else around in a wheelchair, while complaining about the Tories under Margaret Thatcher. Else reacted by turning off her hearing aid. Dandy Nichols was, in fact, seriously ill and died in 1986, but the series continued with Alf as a widower.

Warren Mitchell was born in 1926 over a fish and chip shop in Stoke Newington, London, that had been opened by his Russian grand-mother. He originally intended to be a scientist; it was while training as a navigator in the RAF in Canada that he was urged by Richard Burton to become an actor, and when he left the RAF he trained at RADA. While Garnett was a West Ham football supporter, Mitchell watched Spurs. He kept a Bernese mountain dog and a giant schnauzer, sailed, played tennis and the clarinet. In 1989 he became an Australian.

While he hated fans shouting 'Hey, Alf' after him, he was incensed when a critic, applauding his performance in a National Theatre pro-duction of Arthur Miller's *Death of a Salesman*, bemoaned the years Mitchell had 'wasted' playing Garnett. 'Alf was no less challenging or rewarding a character to play than Willy Loman,' Mitchell wrote to the newspaper. 'Alf Garnett is one of the great dramatic creations of our time. Boorish he may have been on occasion; boring he never was. I love the old bastard.'

Arthur Lowe

Being short, rotund and prematurely bald, Arthur Lowe was always destined to be a character actor rather than a romantic lead. He started losing his hair at 21 and was practically bald at 30. He played many roles but the

★ Arthur Lowe in his greatest role as Capt. Mainwaring in *Dad's Army* and, above, with John Le Mesurier as the always polite, diffident Sergeant Wilson ★

greatest was in *Dad's Army* by Jimmy Perry and David Croft, which began in 1968. He played Captain Mainwaring, a bank manager of Warmington-on-Sea, and commander of its Home Guard platoon.

Mainwaring was pompous, vain, foolish, but he was brave, loyal and well-meaning. 'Steady on, we're not savages,' he would caution over-enthusiastic recruits. His platoon was incompetent but willing. Sgt Wilson (John Le Mesurier), his vague, diffident, public-school educated deputy at the bank, was always querying his orders with, 'Excuse me sir, do you think that's wise?' Mother's boy Private Pike (Ian Lavender) was always fearful of his mother's wrath; 'Stupid boy!' Mainwaring would say witheringly. Most of the others were geriatrics. Lance Corporal Jones (Clive Dunn), the Warmington butcher and a veteran of ancient military campaigns, prefaced every remark with, 'Permission to speak, sir?', urged, 'Don't panic', as he started a panic, and advocated the use of bayonets with the cry, 'They don't like it up them.' Private Fraser, the pessimistic undertaker (John Laurie), cried, 'We're doomed', and Private Godfrey (Arnold Ridley) asked at inopportune moments, 'May I spend a penny?'

Lowe was born at Hayfield, Derbyshire in 1915, the only son of a railway worker, and left school at 16 to work in an aircraft factory. He joined a cavalry regiment before World War Two because he was keen on horses but by 1940 it had been converted to medium artillery. He acquired a taste for acting while serving on Palestine's Gaza Strip where boredom moved the troops to put on plays. After the war, which he ended as a Warrant Officer in REME, he took a course at RADA, then joined a rep company in Manchester. He made his West End debut in 1950 and was in musicals including *Call Me Madam, Pal Joey* and *The Pajama Game.*

His first big role on television was as Leonard Swindley, pompous draper and chairman of the Glad Tidings mission hall, in *Coronation Street* in 1961. This led to a spin-off series, *Pardon the Expression*, in 1965 in which Swindley became assistant manager of a northern chain store. He played Swindley in more than 400 programmes between 1960 and 1965.

After nine years in *Dad's Army* he was successively the crafty Irish priest Father Duddleswell

in *Bless Me Father* and the retired *Potter* in 1979, and *A.J. Wentworth BA*, a prep school maths master, in 1982. The last series was Lowe's legacy to TV, recorded only weeks before he died.

Lowe was a workaholic who never took holidays, though his hobby was a 100-year-old, sea-going, single-funnelled steamboat *Amazon*, which he renovated and equipped with a harmonium. When on board he would don a yachting cap and blazer every evening. He had a dry wit and a streak of grumpiness. 'Being addressed as Swindley or Mainwaring irritated the hell out of me,' he said. 'I wanted to be recognised for myself and not one of the characters I created.'

In 1982 he collapsed in his dressing room in a theatre in Birmingham where he was playing in the comedy *Home at Seven* with his actress wife Joan Cooper and died in hospital.

Reg Varney

Employees of a bus company were the subjects of *On the Buses* in 1969. Writers Ronald Wolfe and Ronald Chesney had been asked for suggestions for a new comedy series after writing *The Rag Trade*, set in a garment factory, and *Meet the Wife*, in a working-class family home. They decided to devise a show which combined situations at work and repercussions at home, and picked on busmen because, they said, when you see a man in a busman's uniform you automatically know an awful lot about him ... how much he earns, the sort of house he might live in.

Reg Varney starred as bus driver Stan Butler with Bob Grant as his conductor, and Stephen Lewis as a harassed Inspector. 'I *hate* you, Butler,' was his cry. A bus depot at London's Wood Green provided the exterior of the headquarters of the Luxton Bus Company from which Butler drove, usually a No. 11 to the cemetery gates. Varney drove the bus himself, although not allowed to carry fare-paying passengers. Despite this, whenever the TV crew put up a dummy request stop in the streets, there would soon be a queue of would-be passengers trying to board. The first *Buses* movie was the most successful British film of 1971.

Varney, only 5 ft 5 in tall and neat, with a wide grin, was born in London's East End. His father was a tyre factory worker. He started to

★ Reg Varney drove a double decker bus as Stan Butler in *On the Buses*, starring in more than 70 episodes and three movies, but after an illness he became one of TV's forgotten stars ★

learn the piano, though he never managed to read music, and as a boy was first on stage in a Russian gypsy outfit, playing *Tiger Rag*. The piano was in the wrong place and his attempts to move it brought his first laughs. At 14 he made his club debut, singing and playing accordion, and at 15 he was singing with big bands. Comedy came later in army concert parties. In the Fifties he was in summer shows and pantos when he was given the part of the foreman in the sitcom, *The Rag Trade*. He went on into *Beggar My Neighbour*.

Varney made more than 70 TV episodes and three films as Stan Butler of *On the Buses*. He then starred in 13 variety shows, and 12 episodes of *Down the Gate*, playing a fish porter in Billingsgate market. He did more than 100 shows for ITV. 'I was never off TV and I began to worry about being seen too often,' he said, so he did stage shows in Australia and New

Zealand. But in 1981 he suffered a coronary, after which he became a forgotten man. Advised to find a pastime during his convalescence, he copied a Corot from a Christmas card with oil paints bought for his daughter but never used by her. He went on to paint landscapes in oils and give exhibitions of his work.

Richard O'Sullivan

There was a new daring about sitcom. As student chef Robin Tripp in *Man About the House* in 1973, Richard O'Sullivan shared a flat with two pretty girls (Paula Wilcox and Sally Thomsett). For O'Sullivan this led to *Robin's Nest* in which Tripp, now a bistro owner, lived with a girlfriend (Tessa Wyatt). For the first time in a British sitcom series it was made plain that a man and girl were living together happily without being married. This had been acceptable in drama but not in a sitcom and the scripts were vetted by the IBA. *Man About the House* had another popular spin-off, *George and Mildred*, which followed the fortunes of George and Mildred Roper, who were Tripp's landlords in *Man About the House*.

O'Sullivan, known to admirers as 'Dishy Dick', possessor of a crooked grin he blames on a cricket ball full in the mouth, was born in 1944 in Chiswick, the son of a garage mechanic. He went to stage school because he wanted to learn to tap dance, and his fellow pupils included Judy and Sally Geeson, Frazer Hines, Francesca Annis and Susan George. He made his film debut at eight as Trevor Howard's son in *The Stranger's Hand* which was filmed in Venice. Then came a string of tear jerkers. He was a crippled child taught to walk again in *Dance Little Lady*, and deaf, dumb and blind in *The Green Scarf*. In his early teens he was well off, then at 16 his voice broke and his income dropped until ITV's *Doctor* series of the Seventies in which he played Dr Bingham.

In *Me and My Girl* in 1984 he played a single-parent advertising executive bringing up a teenage daughter (Joanne Ridley).

John Inman

The part which made John Inman an award-winner in the mid-Seventies was that of Mr Humphries, a camp shop assistant who wanted to take a leg measurement even when selling a shirt, and volunteered his services with a cry of

★ John Inman made his name as a camp shop assistant in *Are You Being Served?* but he can also perform a classy song and dance act with top hat and cane ★

'I'm free'. That was in the BBC's *Are You Being Served?* which began in 1974. Inman played him with limp wrists and a mincing walk, basing him, he said, on shop assistants he had known during a brief time as a window dresser at Austin Reed in the West End.

Inman was born in Preston, Lancashire in 1935. His mother ran a seven-bedroom Blackpool boarding house called Glen Royal, and his father a hairdressing business. He started his career at 13 in a play called *Freda* at Blackpool and at 21 joined a touring rep company. Summer seasons and pantomimes followed and he became an established traditional dame with baskets and crates of dresses, lime green and purple, puce and crimson, lemon and black, all embroidered and trimmed with lace, feathers, net fur or glittering sequins, on which he lavished care. He had learned to sew at the age of seven.

After *Are You Being Served?* he starred in *Take a Letter Mr Jones* in which he was a secretary to whom Rula Lenska dictated.

David Jason

The male sitcom star of the Eighties was David Jason in *Only Fools and Horses*, a title derived from the adage: 'Only fools and horses work.' Jason played Derek Trotter, better known as Del Boy, camel-hair coated and barrow-boy smart, flogging dodgy goods with his dim younger brother, Rodney (Nicholas Lyndhurst). 'You plonker, Rodney,' Del would say as his sibling wrecked a promising scheme. Originally the Trotter household was completed by Granddad (Lennard Pearce), but after that actor's death the character was replaced by old sailor Uncle Albert (Buster Merryfield). Usually such characters as Del are losers, but he was a winner, or at least, a survivor.

Jason, who is only 5 ft 6 in tall, was born David White in 1940, son of a fishmonger and a char, living in Edmonton, London, with an outside loo and a tin bath on a peg by the back door. He began work as a garage mechanic and then was an electrician until he was 26. During this time he appeared in amateur dramatics. 'They kicked cowards but they didn't kick clowns,' says Jason. His brother, actor Arthur White, who was once in *Crossroads*, helped him by introducing him to producers, one of whom gave him his first professional role, in a Bromley production of *South Sea Bubble*.

A Dick Emery season at Bournemouth led to a part in *Do Not Adjust Your Set* and he went on to play in the *Doctor* series, *Lucky Feller, The Top Secret Life of Edgar Briggs* and *A Sharp Intake of Breath*. By this time he was respected by other actors, but was not a star to the public until Ronnie Barker's *Open All Hours*, in which he played Granville, the oldest errand boy in the business.

★ A relaxed and happy Mike Yarwood, who gave impressions a new dimension; in the mid-Eighties, however, he encountered problems ★

★ The Big Yin, Billy Connolly, at the microphone, showing why he was once voted Britain's scruffiest man and his wife, Pamela Stephenson, once Britain's most outrageous woman ★

★ Alas, Mel and Griff were not at their
funniest in their film clip show, *The World
According to Smith and Jones* ★

★ Lenny Henry, the comedian with a
conscience − and a good line in large
suits ★

★ Talented comic, singer and songwriter, Victoria Wood (above). Self-confessed on-stage madman, Russ Abbot (below) ★

★ Proving that comics need not look
comical, the chic and glamorous Marti
Caine (formerly Lynda Crapper) of *New
Faces* ★

★ Penelope Keith, first lady of British sitcoms, delivered cutting lines in *The Good Life*, *To the Manor Born* and *Executive Stress* ★

★ 'Dishy Dick', Richard O'Sullivan, who
played Robin Tripp, student chef in *Man
About the House* and bistro owner in
Robin's Nest ★

★ *Only Fools and Horses* by John Sullivan was the BBC's biggest sitcom hit of the early Eighties, starring David Jason (right) as flash would-be wheeler-dealer Del Trotter, and Nicholas Lyndhurst as his naive younger brother Rodney. In early series they were partnered by Lennard Pearce as Granddad; after his death in 1984 they were joined by Buster Merryfield as Uncle Albert ★

While still appearing as Del Boy he then astonished fans by playing Skullion, a cantankerous, narrow-minded college head porter of pensionable age with greying hair slicked back, Denis Healey eyebrows and a bushy moustache, a starched collar, bowler hat and gold watch and chain in *Porterhouse Blue*. 'I hope people in the business will say, "Blimey, we never thought of him carrying a part like that,"' said Jason, and they did.

He has also provided the clipped upper-crust voice of the cartoon hero *Danger Mouse*, and of Toad in *Wind in the Willows*.

Bill Cosby

The highest-paid sitcom star is, however, America's Bill Cosby, who has made television history leading an all-black cast in *The Cosby Show* since 1984. Earlier American comedies about blacks had tended to stereotype adults as servants and clowns, and children as cute. *The Cosby Show* was the first to concern a middle-class black family.

Cliff Huxtable (played by Cosby) was a New York obstetrician, and his wife Clair (Phylicia Rashad) was a lawyer, and they were raising five children in an enlightened manner. The family, in fact, resembled Cosby's own; he kept photos of his four daughters and son in his dressing room. The series dramatised small domestic crises such as the death of a pet goldfish. Racial issues rarely featured – 'I don't spend hours worrying how to slip a social message into my act,' he says – and most of the scripts could have been played by whites. By 1986 it was the most popular TV show in America.

It was praised for upholding the strength of the American family, for showing that, given education and careers, blacks could rise in society. Coretta Scott King, widow of Martin Luther King, said: 'The show is certainly the most positive portrayal of black family life that has ever been broadcast. With one out of three

★ **Bill Cosby made television history in 1965 when he became the first black to share equal billing in an American TV series with a white actor. That was with Robert Culp in *I Spy*. He made more history in the Eighties with his sitcom series, *The Cosby Show*, by playing an obstetrician, head of a middle-class black family** ★

black families living below the poverty line it is inspiring to see a black family that has managed to escape the violence of poverty through education and unity.'

It was criticised for idealising black life and ignoring racialism, though Harvard psychiatrist Dr Alvin Poussaint, a consultant on the programme whom Cosby telephoned weekly for his views, replied: 'This show is changing the white community's perspective of black Americans. It's doing far more to instil positive racial attitudes than if Bill came at the viewer with a sledgehammer or a sermon.'

The series, of which Cosby was not only the star but co-creator, co-producer and co-writer of the theme song, helped make him America's highest paid entertainer, the owner of a private jet and 15 cars including a Rolls-Royce and an Aston-Martin. (Additional money came from 20 hit record albums and six singles, films, nightclub performances and advertising.)

Cosby was born in Philadelphia in 1937. His father was a ship's steward often at sea, his mother a cleaner. As a boy he shined shoes, played street football, took part in teen gang wars and dropped out of school. He joined the navy as a medical orderly, enrolled in correspondence courses conducted by the navy and belatedly got a high school diploma. He also competed for the navy at athletics as a high jumper, sprinter and footballer and was awarded an athletics scholarship to university. To earn spending money while working for his degree he worked as a bartender, began entertaining customers to pass the time and became a club comedian.

He went from stand-up comic to actor in 1965 in television's *I Spy*, a secret agent series in which he co-starred with Robert Culp, becoming the first black actor to win equal billing in an American series. It was a role in which his colour was immaterial. Three TV stations, two in Georgia and one in Florida, declined to screen it because of his colour, but it won him three Emmy awards.

In *The Bill Cosby Show* from 1969 he played a high school athletics coach and was also executive producer. The black characters were well-rounded and normal; the whites were the deliberate stereotypes. With a doctor's degree in education, Cosby now teaches educational psychology at the University of Massachusetts when he is not entertaining.

★

COMIC ACTRESSES

★

June Whitfield says: 'People don't easily accept a woman comic. For a woman to tell risqué jokes or ones about the mother-in-law is the surest way of losing her femininity overnight.' Women have not often been the stars of situation comedy either, despite the early success of *I Love Lucy*. More commonly they are seen in supporting roles. This does not bother Whitfield. She says: 'I'm happier playing second fiddle to the star.'

June Whitfield

She has been the archetypal sitcom woman, ever the fiancée or loyal wife, notably as June in *Terry and June*. She first worked with Terry Scott in 1969, playing domestic sketches with him in *Scott On . . .* In 1974 they were teamed in *Happy Ever After* as Terry and June Fletcher, whose children had left home and who had different ideas on how to spend their new-found leisure. Five series of *Happy Ever After* have been followed by ten of *Terry and June*, and that title has become a synonym for cosy domestic comedy. A fan once asked her, 'Where's your husband?' When she pointed to Tim Aitchison, a retired surveyor, the fan was scornful: 'I'm talking about your real husband.' He meant, of course, Terry Scott.

A vivacious 5 ft 3 in tall, June Whitfield has never been required or allowed to be neurotic or tragic or sexy; she has always been the Loyal Little Woman, sweet as sugar, clean as washing powder (though she has been able to extend her range in TV commercials as a glamorous spy and an Eastern beauty).

She was born in London. Her father was a Yorkshire businessman and she grew up in an elegant Victorian house in Belgravia with two maids. Her mother started her on elocution, dancing and singing lessons and she went on to RADA, although, on her father's advice, she also took a secretarial course.

She was first heard on radio in 1951 when she was required to make crying baby noises for a programme called *Focus on Nursing*. Then she spent seven years in radio's *Take It From Here*, playing Eth, the perpetual fiancée of Ron Glum with her plaintive cry of, 'Oh, Ron!' She modelled Eth's whining voice on that of a friend of her mother.

She started in TV in the Fifties in *Fast and Loose* with Bob Monkhouse, moved on to *The Seven Faces of Jim* with Jimmy Edwards, and was then in three series of *Beggar My Neighbour* with Peter Jones. She was the nurse in Tony Hancock's *The Blood Donor*. Her actress daughter, Susan Aitchison, has been in two series of Russ Abbot shows, and mother and daughter first appeared together in 1987 in a Roy Hudd show on ITV.

Mollie Sugden

While June Whitfield is the archetypal wife, Mollie Sugden is the mother. She was the mother of Nerys Hughes in *The Liver Birds*, John Alderton in *My Wife Next Door*, Robin Nedwell in the *Doctor* series, Jimmy Clitheroe in *Just Jimmy*, and Christopher Blake in *That's My Boy*, in which she starred as Ida Willis, a char reunited with her long-lost doctor son.

Mother of twins in real life, she appeared with her husband, actor William Moore, in *My Husband and I*, but her best-known role has been with lacquered, high-piled hair as Mrs Slocombe, dragon of the ladies' wear department in *Are You Being Served?*

She was born in 1922 in Keighley, Yorkshire, where her father was a lay preacher and she

★ Hattie Jacques demonstrating hula-hooping during the craze of 1958; she later put on considerably more weight. The versatile actress was formerly married to John Le Mesurier, another sitcom star ★

140

★ June Whitfield, star of *Terry and June*, and right, Mollie Sugden, here seen as Mrs Slocombe in *Are You Being Served?* ★

learned a comic poem watching a woman at a church function. She trained at Guildhall School of Music and Drama and was eight years in rep, before a string of television parts including that of Annie Walker's rival land-lady, Nellie Harvey, licensee of the Laughing Donkey, in the early days of *Coronation Street*. She saw none of them. She never watches herself. She says she is shy.

Miriam Karlin

One of the stronger parts for women was that played by Miriam Karlin in *The Rag Trade*, which began on BBC in the Fifties, and made a brief comeback on ITV in 1977. It was set in a dressmakers' workroom and concerned the never-ending conflict between the boss (Peter Jones) and the workers, represented by husky-voiced Karlin as Paddy, the militant shop steward crying, 'Everybody out!'

She herself has been a militant member of Equity, the actors' union, and was awarded the OBE for union and welfare work. Her father, barrister Henry Samuels, wrote standard works

on trade unions, and in *The Rag Trade*, as Paddy, she often quoted factory acts as set out in her father's book.

She was born in Hampstead and brought up in a traditional Orthodox Jewish way and has campaigned for Jewish and left-wing causes all her life. Some of her mother's family died at Auschwitz. She trained at RADA and went into rep. Standing 5 ft 6 in tall, she was once 11 stone 8 lb in weight – 'enormously fat', she says – but shed two stone in 1956 for a stage role in a Shaw play in which she had to wear trousers, and then became almost anorexic. She once chainsmoked 40 or 50 cigarettes a day but stopped after a smoking and cancer report in 1970.

Hylda Baker

Hylda Baker was a comparative rarity, a stand-up comic who turned actress in sitcoms. In 1968 in *Nearest and Dearest* she played Nellie Pledge, a garrulous know-all running a pickle factory with her lazy, drunken brother Eli. He was played by Jimmy Jewel, a music-hall comic whose 30-year partnership with Ben Warris had come to an end shortly before the series began.

Baker went on to play barmaid Nellie Pickersgill in *Not on Your Nellie*, which was set in a London pub. The joke was that Nellie, who travelled from the North in answer to a plea for help from her licensee father, did not approve of drinking. While looking for a London pub to serve as a model for the television one, Hylda Baker and a member of the production team pub-crawled their way through west London one night. Eventually they found their ideal, but in the morning Baker had a hangover and could not remember its name or location.

Before these sitcoms she had been a music-hall star of the Fifties in an act as a fast-talking gossip with a silent friend, Cynthia, as her stooge. She was born in Farnworth, Lancashire, one of the seven children of Harold Baker, a painter and signwriter who also worked the halls as a comedian. At three she would sing the songs of the day and finish with a clog dance. Before she reached her teens she was topping variety bills as a child prodigy and then her father suggested she ought to learn a trade. Show business was a precarious profession and she might find it tougher as a woman. She found a job in a Bolton clothes factory making off the peg dresses, but stayed only six months. At 14 she was back on stage. However, she had acquired a useful ability. 'It was impossible to hear oneself speak above the noise of the sewing machines,' she said, 'and I soon discovered that the girls solved this problem by mouthing their words and lip-reading. This later proved to be a great asset to me in my act with Cynthia.'

During World War Two she produced and staged her own shows within shows with titles including *Meet the Girls* and *Bearskins and Blushes*, designing the dresses and scenery and on occasion conducting the orchestra. She toured for 15 years, but her productions were always second feature to such stars as Johnny Ray and Guy Mitchell. She wanted to be a big star herself, so she sold the costumes, scenery and props and embarked on a solo career.

It was in 1955 that she created her act as a know-all with a tall, mute friend, Cynthia. Baker stood 4 ft 11 in and was loquacious. Cynthia was 6 ft plus, (played by different men) and dumb. Baker would gossip in the manner of women in fish and chip shop queues, corner shops and pubs, salting her lines with mala-

★ Hylda Baker in her routine as a fast-talking gossip. Her stooge was six-foot-tall Cynthia (played by a man) who never spoke ★

propisms. Cynthia would display no reaction. 'She just looks through yer,' Baker would observe to the audience. 'I wouldn't care, but she knows, y'know.' After a television appearance in *The Good Old Days*, 'She knows, y'know' quickly became a catch phrase. She died in 1986.

Penelope Keith

The first lady of sitcoms in the Seventies was Penelope Keith, mistress of disdainful, snobbish and bitchy roles. *The Good Life* in 1974 was the story of a suburban couple, the Goods (Richard Briers and Felicity Kendal) trying to wrest a living from their garden but the viewers' favourite character was Margo Leadbetter (played by Keith), their disapproving next door neighbour who would never be caught in the same dress two coffee mornings running. 'Poor Margo, she simply will not let well alone, she dresses for positively every occasion,' said Keith at the time. 'Like when she was helping the Goods to harvest the crops, she couldn't just throw on her oldest clothes, she had to go and rig herself out in a yellow sou'wester with matching wellingtons. I felt I looked like some kind of crazy canary. She's snobbish and selfish and tactless, but with a heart of gold . . . more scatty than nasty. Mind you, I wouldn't spend much time with her myself. I once had a girl friend like her, married to a very rich chap, terribly elegant, bored the pants off me, she spent so much time dressing up.'

Laden with awards, Keith went on to star in *To the Manor Born* as Audrey Fforbes-Hamilton, owner of a country manor house which, impoverished in widowhood, she was forced to sell to a rich businessman (Peter Bowles). Originally she despised him for being in trade, but fell for his charm, and the wedding was an eagerly awaited TV event. Keith and Bowles went on to co-star in *Executive Stress* as executives in a publishing firm, married to each other but forced to keep it a secret because the firm had a rule against employing husbands and wives.

Penelope Keith, whose own marriage is to Rodney Timpson, a former policeman, was born in Sutton, Surrey, an only child, but her mother was divorced when she was small and worked in various hotels, and Keith was sent to a boarding school in Sussex at the age of six. She was taken regularly to West End theatres by her mother and grandmother and decided at the age of five to be an acress. She went on to drama school and into rep at Chesterfield where she once had to dye her hair red because the company could not afford a wig. She was in *Emergency – Ward 10* as a casualty.

By her own description, she was 'tall and rather plain'. She says: 'When I was 19 I looked about 93. People kept saying wasn't it wonderful I could play such young girls and get away with it. Not a bad way to begin, because now I can only get younger.'

Su Pollard

Hi-de-Hi! in 1980 was another exercise in nostalgia by Jimmy Perry and David Croft, the writers of *Dad's Army*. It was set in Maplin's, an incompetently staffed holiday camp in the Fifties, and for seven years Su Pollard played scatty chalet maid Peggy Ollerenshaw, yearning to become a Yellowcoat and dump her bucket and mop.

She was born in 1949 in Nottingham where both her parents worked in a cigarette factory, and first became interested in being an actress

at the age of four. She was in her first play, as a fairy, at the age of six, and at 11 she joined an amateur company; she also learned shorthand and typing. She temped for a couple of years, but also did an act in pubs wearing hot pants and tiger-skin boots. In *Opportunity Knocks!* in 1973 she came second to a Jack Russell dog which sang *Oh What a Beautiful Morning*. But she then joined the singers in a touring production of *The Desert Song* and gave up typing. She has a belting voice, and since her success as Peggy has made records; her second, *Starting Together*, reached second place in the charts in 1986.

She has also been in demand for commercials. She co-starred with donkeys in a tea ad and dressed up as a bumble bee in one for an air freshener. 'I don't mind how daft I look,' she says. 'Some comediennes are not prepared to dress up and look silly. I wouldn't mind dressing up as a tree if it was funny.'

Wildly animated, she pulls faces as she talks and throws herself about on a chair. She normally wears gigantic rimmed glasses because she is shortsighted, and says that at a party she once sat on a dog, mistaking it for a stool.

Tracey Ullman

Tracey Ullman appeared in the sitcom *Girls on Top* in 1985 with French and Saunders, playing Candice, a brassy blonde with an imaginary illness and an inability to tell the truth, but Candice was not as memorable as other characters in this chapter. Tracey Ullman is better known as a star of sketch shows, but she insists she is an actress, delivering scripts by others, and not a comedienne, so she may be considered here.

She is best known for her impersonations of daffy debutantes, frumpy housewives, batty barmaids and inarticulate teenagers saying 'okay, soopah, yah, right, okay, yah Roz'. On chat shows she switches characters so quickly that her accents and impersonations trip over one another.

She was born in 1959 in Buckinghamshire. Her father was a wealthy Polish lawyer who had come to Britain as a soldier during the war, and she went to a private school in Chertsey and rode ponies in gymkhanas. But her father died when she was six and her mother, who had never worked, was forced to drive a van for a garage and wash up in pubs, while Ullman had

★ Tracey Ullman, below, in a scene from her 1984 pop video, *My Guy's Mad at Me*, which was shown on Channel 4's *The Tube*; her newspaper-reading stooge is Labour Party leader Neil Kinnock ★

★ Su Pollard, left, as Peggy Ollerenshaw, the holiday camp chalet maid who dreamed of becoming a Yellowcoat, in *Hi-di-Hi!*, pictured with Paul Shane as Ted Bovis, the camp's comic ★

to move to a state school. She was a dumpy child with a lisp and to compensate clowned to make classmates laugh. Her audition choice for admission to a stage school was Stanley Holloway's Lion and Albert monologue. Her first jobs were in musicals and rep; she was an end of the pier dancer and at 16 joined the Second Generation dance troupe. She then switched to drama and won an award as the most promising new actress of 1980 in *Four in a Million* at the Royal Court.

She starred with Lenny Henry and David Copperfield in the BBC's *Three of a Kind* in 1981 and in a memorable sketch sent up *The Benny Hill Show* by pinching male bottoms, looking down men's shirt fronts and leering. At the same time she pursued a pop career with records including *They Don't Know About Us* and the Doris Day classic, *Move Over Darling*. In Hollywood in 1983 she married TV comedy producer, Allan McKeown, the man behind *Auf Wiedersehen, Pet* and *Girls on Top*.

By 1985 she was established as a young comic with a talent for mimicry. *My Guy's Mad at Me*, a pop record she made, was accompanied by a video in which Neil Kinnock appeared. She was

in the movie *Plenty* with Meryl Streep, and said she knew she'd arrived when a readers' poll in *City Limits* voted her the Person You'd Most Like to Spend All Day on Clapham Common With, ahead of Boy George and Pamela Stephenson. But she was unhappy about the opportunities for women comics in Britain, claiming that in *Monty Python* if they wanted a woman they usually had Terry Jones dressed up as one, while in *The Benny Hill Show* they were props.

So she quit Britain for the United States in 1987 when she was offered the chance to star in her own series, *The Tracey Ullman Show*, for American television. Before starting work on the shows she was made to watch videos of Sid Caesar, Ernie Kovacs, Mary Tyler Moore, Lucille Ball and Phil Silvers and assimilate American phrasings and intonations. By the end of the first season the show had been nominated for five Emmy awards. Some fans thought she came from Texas; few were aware she was English, but the programmes were so American in style that British viewers were unimpressed when the first of them were screened by BBC2 in 1988.

145

THE NEW WAVE

★

Alternative comedy is so called because it bars sexist and racist jokes and what its exponents regard as smug, middle-class humour. It began, as far as television is concerned, with the Comic Strip. In 1980 Peter Richardson was performing at the Comedy Store in London's Soho, modelled on similar American clubs. Dozens of comedy acts turned up each night unauditioned and unpaid to entertain, and were barracked by the audience until gonged by the loud-mouthed compere, Alexei Sayle. It was like a Roman lions v Christians fixture.

Richardson decided to open a new venue where new comedians would get the opportunity to perform for a reasonable time and the audience would give them a chance. He got financial backing from impresario Michael White and film producer John Goldstone and found premises above the Raymond Revuebar in Soho, sharing a stage door with the cast of the strip show *Erotica 1981* playing downstairs.

Artists from the Comedy Store were invited and Alexei Sayle went as compere. The show was billed as 'London's newest anarchic cabaret' and its nucleus was three partnerships: the Outer Limits (Peter Richardson and Nigel Planer), 20th Century Coyote (Rik Mayall and Adrian Edmondson) and Dawn French and Jennifer Saunders. They were new in that they were neither from Oxbridge revues nor northern clubs but from a variety of backgrounds and places, sharing little more than their sense of humour. They were not alone in that. The Comic Strip was packed every night, and as word spread White commissioned the first TV production from the team.

The first of *The Comic Strip Presents . . .* was screened on Channel 4 on its opening night in 1982 and was *Five Go Mad in Dorset*, a parody of Enid Blyton. 'Four famous brats and a dog have a ripping time on their summer hols' ran the blurb. 'Their self-righteous sleuthing leads them into perilous scrapes and wizard wheezes.' It starred Ade Edmondson, Dawn French, Peter Richardson and Jennifer Saunders in shorts and ankle socks, cycling along leafy lanes, eating enormous teas and displaying prep school snobbery. 'Ooh, what a horrid, common voice that man has,' they said, and 'How can we let Toby be our friend, Dick? We don't even know if he goes to a good school.' More *Comic Strip Presents* followed, each one caricaturing a different film stereotype.

There was a vacuum in TV comedy in the early Eighties. Established comics were moving into game shows. The *Monty Python* team had gone into films. Comedy was represented mainly by impressionists and sitcoms. The ten members of the team filled the gap, dominating the output of British humour in TV, films (of which *Supergrass* was the first in 1984), books and records. The artists surfaced all over TV, grouping and regrouping in different programmes and intermarrying. In one week in 1985 members of the Comic Strip were responsible for the best-selling book, the number one record and the highest-rating youth programme on television. They were called the *Carry On* team of the Eighties.

'Outrageous, provocative, irreverent,' raved the critics, some meaning it as praise, others as condemnation. The comics affected disinterest. They had a distaste for the press. Adrian Edmondson said: 'We consciously adopt a dislike of the press. We all think what we do is more interesting than what we talk about.'

Alexei Sayle

As performers the most successful since include Alexei Sayle who appeared in his solo act threatening vandalism and assault, a bald, bulky, belligerent man in a too-tight suit which

★ Spearhead of the new wave of alternative comedians was the bald and burly, ranting, roaring Alexei Sayle, a former lecturer who was discovered at London's Comedy Store ★

147

he told audiences he bought at a shop for the fuller figure – Mr Fat Bastard. He described his stage character as 'The sort of bloke who got put into prison for GBH at the height of the Mod era and got 23 A-levels and a degree in sociology while he was inside, and then they let him out in 1980 and gave him his old suit back. After all that prison food it couldn't ever fit.'

A verbal hooligan, he wielded humour like a thug with a pick handle, ranting and roaring. One reporter claimed to have counted 50 swearwords in two minutes. He was as rude about Neil Kinnock as Margaret Thatcher. 'If I'd wanted a bald Harold Wilson I'd have asked for one.' He fulminated against medallion men, colour supplement apartments with stripped pine furniture, Jaguars with mink steering wheel gloves, Princess Diana lookalikes called Fiona, and the Social Democrats. 'Isn't it wonderful to see people with acute brain damage forming their own party?' He attacked modern architecture, cocktail bars, fascists, college lecturers, yoghurt eaters, 2CV drivers, working-class peers, Habitat shoppers, cats and social workers, launching a 'Help a London kid; kill a social worker' campaign'.

In one routine he was going to visit the Hayward Gallery to see an exhibition, the Retrospective of Futurist Painting, but called in a pub to ask the way, got into an academic argument with the barman about fine points of Futurist art, and ended the debate by head butting him. In the BBC's *The Young Ones* he played several parts, a psychotic axe-wielding landlord and various relatives – Billy (who was mental), Tommy (a drunk), Ronny (criminal) and Keith (homicidal). 'I come in for five minutes, shout and go out. I'm not part of the plot, more a diversion,' he explained.

Of the raw anger he displayed in his performances, he said: 'I don't bottle it up or go out and get drunk or get into fights in the street. I store it up and use it all on stage. There are just a million things that make me angry but I'm not like the geezer I play on stage; if I was I'd be out killing people.' He admitted that 'People think of me as a cross between Sid Vicious and Bernard Manning', but privately journalists have found him quiet, hesitant and unassuming.

He was brought up in Liverpool and named Alexei in honour of maternal grandparents who left Russia before World War One. His father was a Manx Communist railwayman, his mother a Jewish Lithuanian who worked for a football pool company. They took their holidays in Eastern bloc countries and Sayle accompanied them on NUR trade delegations, visiting Czech ballbearing factories and Rumanian transport depots.

He studied at Chelsea College of Art – drawing horses, tanks and guns, he says – and became a freelance illustrator. Later he taught general studies as a part-time lecturer at London colleges until the start of the Comedy Store. After answering an ad in *Private Eye* he taught all day and went to the Store at night where he derided other comics before banging a gong to end their acts.

He gave up stand-up comedy in 1985 because he found it constricting and he was tired of shouting. He played a heavy in the films *Gorky Park* and *Siesta*, and appeared at the Old Vic as Trinculo, the jester in *The Tempest*. He took up weight training and attended classes in martial arts and dancing and by 1988 when he starred in a BBC TV series, *Alexei Sayle's Stuff*, he had shed two stone of his former 17-stone weight. That series revealed a new Sayle; he played different characters in sketches, and sang and danced.

Mayall, Edmondson and Planer

Rik Mayall and Adrian Edmondson had met at Manchester University, became friends and did shows together. In the Comic Strip they worked with Nigel Planer, who had dropped out of African and Asian studies at Sussex University and gone on to drama school. In the BBC's *The Young Ones* in 1982, a schoolboyish nose-thumbing romp, they came together as the members of an unsavoury household of eternal students and drop-outs, screaming and head banging.

Mayall played Spotty Rick, Edmondson was Violent Vyvyan, a punk, and Planer was Neil, a lank-haired, whining hippy, into love and lentils and refusing to use wooden cocktail sticks because of the trees. 'We wanted to show how unlikeable people are,' said Planer. 'So much is focused on young people but they're never really shown as horrible as they are.' Older viewers thought the series did just that, but it was followed with delight by younger ones. It ran for three seasons and spawned three best-selling books and two hit records by Planer as

★ Nigel Planer as Neil, the hairy hippy in 1984. He later discarded the character saying, 'Neil is an unpleasant, self-pitying bastard.' (above) ★

★ Rik Mayall as the unscrupulous, self-seeking Alan B'Stard MP in *The New Statesman* in 1987 (right) ★

Neil, who had previously been a character he played in stand-up comedy. When Planer decided to finish with Neil he said: 'I'm not sorry to see him go. Although he has a following of people who think he is nice because he is so downtrodden, Neil is an unpleasant, self-pitying bastard.'

Mayall, Edmondson and Planer then went into *Filthy Rich and Catflap*, a send-up of the nature of celebrity, with Mayall as Richie Rich, a television nonentity whose ambition was to read the gossip on breakfast TV. It was hammered by critics for being rude and unfunny, and *Hardwicke House* in 1987 got an even worse reception. It was set in a school with Roy Kinnear as the drunken headmaster and Mayall and Edmondson as two former pupils fresh out of Borstal. The series caused such a public outcry it was terminated after only two of its seven episodes.

Since then Mayall has had a hit as smarmy MP Alan B'Stard in *The New Statesman*. 'He is to democracy what the Beastie Boys are to chamber music,' wrote one critic. B'Stard was avaricious, unscrupulous, cowardly and bullying, an entrepreneur who sold faulty firearms to the police and whose role in politics was to shout 'Go back to Russia', when Labour MPs spoke, and to ask questions designed to start rumours about shares from which he could benefit. But Mayall no longer pranced about breaking wind and some viewers thought him handsome when he did not contort his features. 'I wanted to make him ugly,' he has confessed. 'I want to make all my characters ugly. Whenever I play someone I disapprove of I make him ugly, but they said, "Stop pulling faces and be cool."'

Edmondson has co-written mass-selling books such as *How to Be a Complete Bastard* with advice on 'How to Hold your Own Kamikaze Death Rally', 'How to Start World War Three with a Bag of 10p Pieces' and 'How to Expose Yourself without Getting Arrested'.

Planer has starred in the sitcom, *Roll Over Beethoven*, as a former heavy metal bass player and in *King and Castle* as a martial arts expert hired to collect debts for an agency. He has also co-written a book, *I, an Actor*, under the name Nicholas Craig, which sent up the acting profession. It was serialised by Radio 4.

French and Saunders

Dawn French and Jennifer Saunders, other founder members of the Comic Strip, first met at the Central School of Speech and Drama while training to become drama teachers. 'For the first year of the course we hated each other,' says French. 'I'd just come back from America and was grotesquely Americanised. I used to wear baseball caps all day and say "gross", "tacky" and "cookies". Eventually though we ended up doing cabaret together.' They spent another two years writing and performing together before joining the Comic Strip in 1980. 'We started when there were a lot of

★ Jennifer Saunders, wife of Adrian Edmondson and partner of Dawn French. In *Happy Families* she played five roles, a grandmother and her four granddaughters. And Edmondson appeared as her grandson ★

★ French and Saunders were founder
members of the Comic Strip. In the Comic
Strip production *Consuela* on Channel 4
French played a sinister housekeeper ★

pro-feminist hard hitting acts about,' says Saunders, 'but we didn't do that – which was to our advantage.'

They wrote and starred in the first of two series of *Girls on Top* for ITV in 1985, playing lodgers in a Chelsea house owned by an eccentric novelist (Joan Greenwood). French played Amanda, a bossy feminist pretending to hate men. Saunders played Jennifer who lived on the sofa in the sitting room and was reckoned the most boring girl in Britain. The others were Tracey Ullman as Candice and Ruby Wax as Shelley, a vulgar American.

In the same year they made *Happy Families* for the BBC. Saunders was ageing grandmother Edith Fuddle, seeking a reunion with her four granddaughters. Her callow grandson, Guy (Ade Edmondson), was entrusted with the task of finding them, and duly did so. Madelaine was a French Bohemian, Roxanne a jailbird, Joyce a novice nun, and Cassie a soap opera star. Saunders played all four, sometimes simultaneously by means of a split screen. 'The idea was for a kind of modern day *Kind Hearts and Coronets*,' she said. 'We filmed it on location in exotic Derbyshire and managed to come up with four very different styles for each grand-daughter. The Madelaine episode was pale, pastel and arty, the jail story like a docu-mentary, the convent one with a jolly Forties feel to it, and Cassie was in the style of a soap opera.'

In their own series, *French and Saunders*, on BBC since 1987, Saunders bullies and belittles French, who stands only a fraction over 5 ft tall, in sketches which have shown them as fat men, body-builders, ballerinas, chambermaids, children and, on one occasion, Elizabeth Taylor (French) and Liza Minnelli (Saunders). French is married to Lenny Henry; Saunders to Adrian Edmondson.

Ben Elton

Ben Elton was not a member of the Comic Strip but wrote or co-wrote much of its members' material including *The Young Ones*, *Filthy Rich and Catflap* and *Happy Families*. He has also been a scriptwriter of *Blackadder* for Rowan Atkinson. He became a solo performer on TV in *Saturday Live* in 1985.

Elton's father is a professor, his mother was a teacher. As a drama student at Manchester University he wrote 11 plays. One was about a

Nazi vicar in the Thirties who was rabidly anti-semitic and produced *The Merchant of Venice* with Shylock as the only Christian and all the other characters Jewish. Mayall and Edmondson were friends at Manchester and when he left he became, like them, a stand-up comic. In the first series of *Saturday Live*, which was hosted each week by different stars including Peter Cook and Pamela Stephenson, he was booked for a five-minute spot, did ten and became resident compere of the next series.

He was dubbed Breathless Ben because of his fast-speaking. Dressed in a glittery suit, he leapt from target to target, from the *Sun* newspaper's obsession with the Duchess of York's weight, to the idea that fast food is destroying all life on earth. He joked about tampons and Shake'n'Vac commercials and using public loos – 'sitting there, petrified that a stranger might hear one go plop'. He says: 'I talk about things that happen in my world, whether it be treading in dog's mess, unemployment or fighting for a double seat on the train.'

He was branded a 'Leftie' comic. 'Ben Elton has made a name for himself as the ranting, raving, loud-mouthed, left-wing voice of com-edy,' said the *Sun* in 1987. 'No subject is too sensitive for his scathing wit, no middle-aged comedian escapes his sharp tongue – and he hates your No. 1 *Sun!*'

He denied the left-wing tag, saying he did not try to be political. 'Politics only emerges in my acts because it's a part of life,' he said. However, he was happy to agree to 'anti-racist' and 'anti-sexist'. 'I saw a gag on TV where this bloke said, "We're all proud to be British. We got the Falklands back, we'll be getting Birmingham and London back next." Now as far as I'm concerned that's illegal, and yet people criticise me for doing the odd toilet gag.'

When Jasper Carrott told a gag about women drivers, Elton followed him on stage saying, 'Nice one, Jasper, really taking on the dangerous controversial issues in your com-edy.' And he has publicly denounced the editor of the *Daily Star* for his use of nude photographs: 'He should be put in prison for his crimes against women.' On stage he is sharp tongued, offstage polite and friendly.

Stephen Fry and Hugh Laurie

'We were never part of the so-called alternative comedy scene, we were still in bed at the time,'

says Stephen Fry, speaking for himself and his partner, Hugh Laurie. However, one or other or both of them have appeared in *The Young Ones, Filthy Rich and Catflap, Happy Families, Blackadder* and *Saturday Live*.

They met at Cambridge in a *Footlights Revue* in 1981 and have been writing and performing together ever since. They went with the revue to Edinburgh and then to Australia, another member of the cast being Emma Thompson. Back in England, no longer students, Fry, Laurie and Thompson were signed by Granada for a series called *Alfresco* in which they were teamed with three other newcomers, Robbie

★ **Ben Elton**, writer of many alternative comedy shows including *The Young Ones*, is also a stand-up comic nicknamed **Breathless Ben** because of his fast delivery of material that shocked many viewers ★

Coltrane, Siobhan Redmond (later in *Bulman*) and Ben Elton.

In 1985, after two series of *Alfresco*, Fry went into a play at Chichester where between performances he revised the old musical *Me and My Girl* which became a hit in London and New York, and has also been seen in Tokyo, Budapest and Australia. It has earned him

★ Hugh Laurie, left, and Stephen Fry, right, have been writing and performing together since they first met at Cambridge in a university revue. They were in *Alfresco* and *Carrott Confidential* before achieving their own series, *A Bit of Fry and Laurie*. They have also starred together in commercials ★

★ Stephen Fry has no need to work. His script for the stage musical *Me and My Girl* has earned him a fortune, and he has also written plays. But he works seemingly non-stop in partnership with Laurie and also solo and on radio ★

enough to retire on, but instead of retiring he worked with Laurie in *Saturday Live* and this led to their own BBC series, *A Bit of Fry and Laurie*. 'More comedy, more incredibly humorous moments,' said Fry. 'To take away and treasure,' added Laurie. 'To wrap in lavender paper and keep in the bottom drawer of one's heart,' ended Fry. They have also made many commercials together.

Harry Enfield

The cult comic of 1987 who made his name in *Saturday Live* was Harry Enfield in the guise of Stavros, a naive Greek kebab house owner who had come to England in the Macmillan era of 'never had it so good'. Enfield based Stavros on the owner of a kebab shop near his then home in Hackney. Unshaven Stavros had only a slight command of English. 'Cor blimey, peeps,' he said – he called everyone peeps which was his abbreviation for people – 'What's he think

he's on about, old Micmallan? I tell you what, peeps. You don't have it so bloody good now.' He featured regularly in the first series of *Saturday Live* and returned by popular demand in the second. When the programme ended the audience brandished cards reading, 'Come Back Stavros' and 'Cheerio Peeps.'

Enfield went on to present an even more popular character, Loadsamoney, a flash, philistine Cockney. Enfield had invented him years earlier to amuse a friend, inspired by oafish yuppies boasting about their birds and their cars in his local on a Friday night. When he heard of London football crowds taunting northern supporters for their poverty, the character adopted the habit of thrusting his money in the faces of the unemployed and sneering 'Loadsamoney'. When he had made a name with Stavros, Enfield incorporated Loadsamoney into his act, wearing a sweatshirt and bleached jeans. 'Loadsamoney' became the

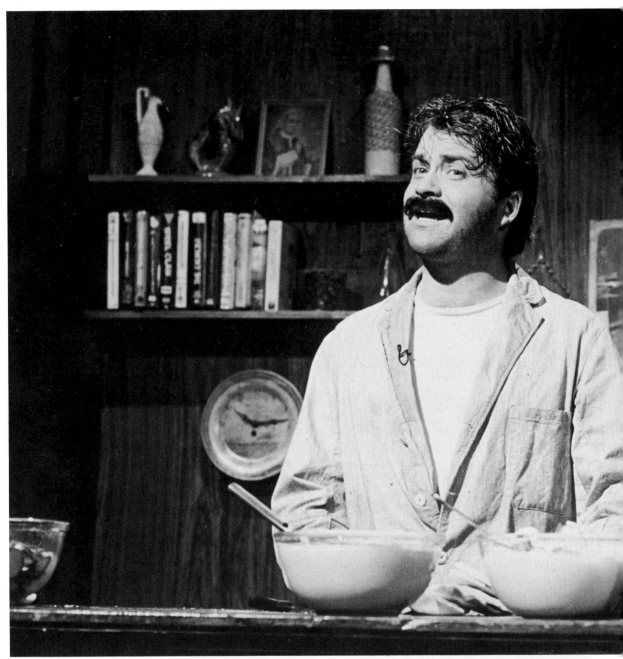

★ Harry Enfield, the cult comic of the late eighties, in his two most famous guises — Stavros, a Greek kebab house owner (above) and the egregious Cockney, Loadsamoney, pictured right with his own brand of 'dosh'. Enfield has also been the voice of many on *Spitting Image* ★

made people laugh.' He read politics at York university but, he says: 'I realised I wasn't going to get a career in politics so I went for the next best thing – comedy. I became one half of a double act called Dusty and Dick, and we toured round the fringe theatres.'

He appeared at the Comedy Store and in cabaret and in 1985 was hired to provide voices for *Spitting Image*. He impersonated David Steel, Denis Norden, Sir Geoffrey Howe, Douglas Hurd, Ken Livingstone, Derek Jameson, Terry Wogan, Frank Bruno and Jimmy Hill. Then came *Saturday Live* and Stavros.

And in conclusion

Dawn French has said: 'Alternative comedy – what does it mean? Either you're funny or you're not.' But for all that is written about alternative or new wave comedians and the shock waves they have caused, the audiences for some of the most publicised shows have been modest. *The Young Ones* was watched by 5.7 million, *Filthy Rich and Catflap* by 3.26 million, *Saturday Live* by 2.2 million for the first series and only 1.5 million for the second. *Gardeners' World* gets bigger audiences. Monkhouse and Tarbuck can draw around 11 million with game shows and popular sitcoms have reached 12 million.

There are good reasons for TV backing alternative comics. It wants to woo the 16½ million young viewers in the 15 to 34 age group. It also wants to develop new comedians. 'There is nowhere for young comics to be bad,' George Burns once complained, though whether TV should provide it is arguable. However, the producers of alternative comedy shows are unabashed by the ratings. 'It's a stupid question to ask why we don't get 13 million viewers because we're not trying to,' Paul Jackson, producer of *The Young Ones* and other alternative series, has said. 'Look at the times they are going out. You can't really win because people define alternative comedy as those shows which attract relatively small audiences. As soon as any programme that comes out of our camp starts to do well, like *Spitting Image, Three of a Kind* or *Carrottt's Lib*, they're called mainstream.'

That is true. Today's alternative comedy becomes tomorrow's mainstream. Television comedy has changed greatly over the years. What will succeed today's is anybody's guess.

most popular catch phrase in the country. 'People like to do impressions of comedians and this is the easiest impression of all,' said Enfield. 'You just shout "Loadsamoney". Anyone can do it.' The word also appeared in advertisements in every local newspaper.

Enfield was raised in Sussex, the son of a local government officer. 'I was fat as a child and used to get assaulted,' he says. 'There were lots of bullies and I had to learn to get on the right side of them to stop them attacking me, so I

157

INDEX

★

Abbot, Russ 99 – 100
Allen, Dave 13 – 14
Askey, Arthur 63 – 4
Atkinson, Rowan 112

Baker, Hylda 142 – 3
Ball, Bobby 18 – 20
Ball, Lucille 52 – 4
Barker, Ronnie 7, 22 – 4, 128
Bass, Alfie 58 – 9
Baxter, Stanley 34 – 5
Benny, Jack 60 – 63, 80
Bentine, Michael 69, 71 – 2
Bootsie and Snudge 58 – 9
Bowen, Jim 94 – 5
Bowles, Peter 144
Brambell, Wilfrid 122 – 4
Bremner, Rory 120 – 1
Burns, George 60
Bygraves, Max 10, 67

Cannon, Tommy 18 – 20
Carrott, Jasper 14 – 15
Carson, Frank 7, 90, 92
Cleese, John 108 – 9
Comic Strip, The 146, 150
Connolly, Billy 38 – 40, 115
Cook, Peter 7, 104, 106 – 8, 109
Cooper, Tommy 7, 74 – 6
Corbett, Harry H 122 – 4
Corbett, Ronnie 22 – 4
Cosby, Bill 139

Davidson, Jim 6, 103
Davro, Bobby 118 – 9
Dawson, Les 96 – 8
Dennis, Les 119 – 120
Dodd, Ken 11 – 13
Drake, Charlie 78 – 80

Edmondson, Adrian 146, 148 – 150
Edwards, Jimmy 57, 64 – 6
Elton, Ben 152
Emery, Dick 33 – 4, 59
Enfield, Harry 154 – 7
Everage, Dame Edna 30 – 2
Everett, Kenny 40, 49

Forsyth, Bruce 77, 82 – 5, 87
Fraser, Bill 58 – 9
French, Dawn 146, 150 – 2, 157
Frost, David 104 – 6, 109
Fry, Stephen 152 – 4
Fyffe, Patrick 28 – 30

Goodies, The 110 – 2
Goodwin, Ken 91 – 2
Grayson, Larry 35 – 7

Hale, Gareth 24 – 7
Hancock, Tony 7, 67 – 9
Henderson, Dickie 54 – 5, 82
Henry, Lenny 98 – 9
Hill, Benny 77 – 8, 79
Hinge and Bracket 28 – 30
Howerd, Frankie 8 – 11
Humphries, Barry 30 – 2

Inman, John 127 – 8

Jacques, Hattie 55 – 6, 68
James, Sid 68
Jason, David 128 – 139
Jones, Griff Rhys 112, 113 – 14

Karlin, Miriam 142
Keith, Penelope 143 – 4

Laurie, Hugh 152 – 4
Large, Eddie 20 – 1
Little, Syd 20 – 1
Logan, George 28 – 30
Lowe, Arthur 125 – 6
Manning, Bernard 90 – 1
Mayall, Rik 146, 148 – 150
Milligan Spike 6, 69 – 71, 73, 85
Mitchell, Warren 7, 124 – 5
Monkhouse, Bob 80 – 1, 82, 85, 87, 90, 96
Monty Python's Flying Circus 108
Moore, Dudley 7, 104, 106 – 8
Morecambe, Eric 7, 16 – 18

Norden, Denis 7

O'Connor, Des 86 – 7
O'Connor, Tom 94
O'Sullivan, Richard 127

Pace, Norman 24 – 7
Planer, Nigel 146, 148 – 150
Pollard, Su 144

Rivers, Joan 50 – 1
Rowan and Martin 88 – 90

Saunders, Jennifer 146, 150 – 2
Sayle, Alexei 146 – 8
Scott, Terry 57, 140
Secombe, Sir Harry 6, 69, 72 – 3, 85
Silvers, Phil 57 – 8
Smith, Mel 112, 113 – 4
Starr, Freddie 49 – 50, 57, 90
Stephenson, Pamela 40, 112, 114 – 5
Sugden, Mollie 140 – 2
Sykes, Eric 6, 10, 55 – 7
Tarbuck, Jimmy 7, 55, 67, 86 – 7

Ullman, Tracey 144 – 5

Varney, Reg 126 – 7
Vaughan, Norman 85, 87

Walker, Roy 6
Whitfield, June 70, 140
Williams, Charlie 90, 92 – 4
Winters, Mike and Bernie 27
Wisdom, Norman 76
Wise, Ernie 16 – 18
Wood, Victoria 7, 100 – 1

Yarwood, Mike 116 – 8, 120